SAGE ADVISOR

Dr. REX JULIAN
BEABER J.D. Ph.D.

Copyright © 2019 Rex Julian Beaber

Sage Advisor/Rex Julian Beaber —1st ed.

All rights reserved. No part of this publication may be reproduced or transmitted in any form or by any means, including photocopying, recording, or other electronic or mechanical methods, without the written permission of the publisher, except in the case of brief quotations embodied in critical reviews and certain other non-commercial uses permitted by copyright law. For permission requests, please contact the author at Xerxers@aol.org or go to http://www.sageadvisor.org

The content in this book solely represents the opinions of the author. Neither the publisher nor the author is engaged in rendering professional advice or services to the individual reader. The ideas and suggestions contained in this book are not intended as a substitute for consulting with your physician, attorney, or other relevant professional.

Cover image is open source.

ISBN-13: 978-1-7332426-0-8
ISBN-10: 1-7332426-0-0:

CONTENTS

	Preface	1
1	WISDOM I.Q. TEST	4
2	WISDOM I.Q. - SCORING	15
3	INTRODUCTION	23
4	COMMON SENSE	31
5	CRITICAL LIFE DECISIONS	35
6	THE TEMPORAL PERSPECTIVE	39
7	WORK, SUCCESS, AND ACHIEVEMENT	42
8	SLEEP	58
9	HEALTH AND BODILY WELLBEING	64
10	FOOD AND EATING	72
11	LOVE, ROMANCE, AND MARRIAGE	75
12	SEX	81
13	FAMILY	86
14	IMPORTANT SKILLS AND KNOWLEDGE	90
15	MONEY AND PERSONAL FINANCE	93
16	FRIENDS	99
17	BOOKS	103

18	CHILDREN	106
19	DIVORCE	111
20	DRUGS AND ALCOHOL	117
21	HOBBIES, RECREATION, AND PLEASURE	121
22	TRAVEL AND VACATION	123
23	EDUCATION	128
24	IDENTIFICATION, DOCUMENTS, AND SAVING THINGS	132
25	LEGAL AFFAIRS	135
26	LYING AND DECEIT	140
27	RELIGION	143
28	MISCELLANEOUS THOUGHTS, OBSERVATIONS, AND RULES	146
29	USEFUL QUOTATIONS	147
30	ABOUT THE AUTHOR	152

Dr. Rex Julian Beaber

PREFACE

This is a book of pragmatic wisdom. I use the term "pragmatic wisdom" because the views expressed in this text are not based on universal truths that are abstract and linked to some well-articulated philosophy or religion. The advice that is given in this work is practical and based on a hodgepodge of experience, psychological insight, patchwork philosophy, and intuitive thoughts. Furthermore, the views that I express in this text are directed toward people who live in a relatively modern culture. There is no wisdom here for an African tribesman or a pauper on the mainland of China. It is in this sense that the direction I offer is not universal and abstract.

It is essential to understand that the recommendations made in this book are probabilistic. That is, they are offered because I think that they usually, or most often, will result in a better life. Necessarily, some of the advice will be bad advice for you because of the chance vicissitudes of life. For example, generally if a woman or man has an affair early during their marriage, while they have young children, it will produce a life filled with misery and difficulty. This being said, sometimes such an affair will lead to the development of a new relationship that fosters a lifetime of happiness.

Accordingly, occasionally following good advice will not lead you down the most perfect life path. The pathways of life, like a fine game of chess, are extremely complex. An apparently faltering foolish move can result in what appears to be a dazzling brilliance in the struggle of happiness.

Life, like chess or backgammon, involves making a series of decisions which impact how your life will be experienced or flow, and, very importantly, what future decisions will need to be made. Some decisions appear trivial and are trivial. For example, deciding what to have for dessert at a restaurant this evening would appear to be a trivial decision having little impact on your total life happiness and direction. Typically, such a decision would in fact be trivial. Nevertheless, there are times when an apparently trivial decision can have a momentous impact on your life. If you, by happenstance, decide to do your laundry and discover that your washing machine is broken, and then decide to go to a laundromat, instead of waiting for a repairman, and then at the laundromat you meet the man or woman of your dreams who you eventually marry, then an apparently trivial decision has changed the course of your life. It is equally true that a decision can appear to be critical, which, ultimately, will have no substantial impact on the quality of your life.

If any given advice is probabilistic and potential fatally defective, why follow any advice? The reason is simple. If you keep ignoring the dictates of generic wisdom, essentially betting that your life or circumstances are an exception to the general rules, it is virtually inevitable that you will suffer dramatic and painful consequences. On average, good advice should be followed because, over a lifetime, it gives you the best chance for happiness. Interestingly, many people already have a good sense of the common-sense rules of happy living. These same people often ignore their own knowledge succumbing to their delusional belief that they have analyzed their circumstances well enough to determine that they fall within an exception. Generally, all people, and especially bright and educated people, overestimate their own ability to predict life events, and they overestimate their skill in navigating around the basic rules of life. Sometimes the most important discipline in life is the ability to curb your own attempts at circumnavigating the basic rules of happiness.

This text is not written as a sequential narrative. That is, it is not written with the idea that it would be read from beginning to end, one chapter after another. Instead, the ideas I am sharing are set forth in different chapters which might be read alone, or in any order. Certainly, the chapters are not in order of importance. Each chapter contains some initial narrative thoughts which do not completely cover the field. The narrative thoughts are followed by directives, i.e., highly specific rules for living. I do not attempt to offer detailed explanations of each rule. In this introductory text, my goal is to simply disseminate the basic rules with an overview of their place in the scheme of life. Indeed, I must confess that I would be unable to justify all the directives, except to say that it is my experience that they work for real people in the real world. Finally, after the last directive in each chapter there is a place for your commentaries, suggestion, and/or critique. Anything written will be read and seriously considered.

1 WISDOM I.Q. TEST

Answer all the questions below before looking at any of the answers in the next chapter. Take as absolutely true any assumption you are given. Choose only one answer. Write down your answer, with the question number, and follow the score instructions in the next chapter.

1. When considering a life choice, you should:
(a) Consider the immediate consequences in terms of pleasure and pain, and always choose the alternative that gives the highest level of immediate pleasure;
(b) Consider the long-term consequences in terms of pleasure and pain, and always choose the alternative that gives the highest level of pleasure over the long run;
(c) Consider the impact of the choice on your family and friends, and choose the alternative that brings them the greatest level of pleasure;
(d) Consider both the short term and long-term consequences in terms of pleasure and pain, and try to strike a balance insuring some pleasure now with good chances for pleasure in the long run;
(e) Consider the instructions in your chosen religion and follow them strictly.

2. Assume you are considering getting one of three of tattoos. One tattoo says: "Make Love Not War". Another tattoo says: "I Love [name of your current lover]." The third tattoo says: "Legalize Marijuana Now." All three tattoos equally and correctly reflect your true sentiments. Which tattoo should you choose?
  (a) "Make Love Not War";
  (b) "I Love XX";
  (c) "Legalize Marijuana Now"

3. Which of the following is a critical life decision:
  (a) What major you declare during your first two years of college;
  (b) When to have your first child;
  (c) What make and model car you will buy when you buy your first new car;
  (d) How to invest in your investment portfolio (i.e., what stocks, bonds, cash accounts, etc.), prior to age 35;

4. The best time to make your final and committed choice about your occupation is:
  (a) In your senior year of high school;
  (b) After two years of college, or age 21 if you do not attend college;
  (c) At age 30;
  (d) At age 35;

5. Assume that you want to be very very wealthy (not just well to do), and that has always been your strong desire. Which is the best route to actualizing your dreams:
  (a) Get a High School Diploma
  (b) Get a B.A. degree;
  (c) Get a law degree (J.D.)
  (d) Get a medical degree (M.D.)
  (e) Get a Ph.D. in psychology
  (f) Get an MBA (master's in business

administration)

6. Assume that you have the raw talent to perform the duties of the occupations listed below better than 90% of the general population. Which occupation should you train for, or prepare for, during your lifetime:
    (a) professional athlete
    (b) rock star
    (c) ballet dancer
    (d) actor
    (e) sculptor
    (f) plastic surgeon

7. Assume that you are working at a job where you have been employed for several years. The job is boring, you do not seem to be advancing, and your immediate supervisor is abusive. What should you do?
    (a) Tell your supervisor that if the abuse does not stop, you will quit;
    (b) Quietly find another job and then quit;
    (c) Quit immediately and seek another job;
    (d) Wait until you have worked for three years and then reassess;
    (e) Tolerate the boredom and seek counseling about the job stress;
    (f) Sabotage your supervisor with an aim of getting him fired and denigrate him to your fellow employees and other supervisors.

8. Assume that you are a fully qualified deep-water welder (repairing ships and underwater pipelines) and making a good living. Your employer has a program for senior employees that will allow you to take fully paid classes one day every two weeks, or a day off, at your choice. What should you do?
    (a) Take a course in business administration;
    (b) Take the time off;

(c) Take a course in advanced welding techniques;
(d) Take a course in art appreciation;
(e) Sue your employer for age discrimination.

9. Assume you are in good financial shape, and you are offered two different jobs, both in your line of work and very interesting. One job requires that you work a late-shift, such that you will not leave work until 2:00 a.m. several days a week. This job pays 15% more than the second job, which has regular work hours. What would you do?

(a) Attempt to bargain for higher wages in the more regular hourly employment;
(b) Seek legal representation on the issue of an emotionally destructive work environment;
(c) Take the better paying job with difficult hours and train yourself to adapt;
(d) Take the more regular employment and live with lower compensation.

10. Which of the following is the most dangerous, from a health point of view? Which is the second most dangerous? Two answers are required here:

(a) Taking 1,000 I.U. of Vitamin D3 a day for supplementation;
(b) Riding as a passenger on a motorcycle;
(c) Allowing a surgeon with poor interpersonal skills and a bad "bedside manner" to perform important surgery on your heart or brain;
(d) Regularly smoking cannabis (marijuana) twice a week;
(e) Ignoring a new lesion (growth) on your arm that is dark with varying shades of black and grey, has irregular borders, and is rough and elevated.

11. Which of the following will make the largest contribution to a long and healthy life span?

(a) Avoiding occupations and hobbies where

you'll be exposed to chemical fumes;

(b) Avoiding the regular use of laxatives and non-prescription drugs;

(c) Having regular physical exams and health maintenance screenings after age 40;

(d) Avoiding ever smoking cannabis (marijuana);

(e) Taking a general vitamin every day.

12. Which approach to eating is the best?

(a) Only eat when you are very hungry.

(b) Adopt a vegan diet.

(c) Eat four to five small meals a day rather than two or three larger meals.

(d) Don't drink green tea or coffee.

(e) Don't drink regular tap water.

13. Which of the following is the best candidate for marriage:

(a) alcoholic;

(b) drug abuser:

(c) policeman;

(d) medical interns;

(e) recently divorced (1 month ago);

(f) mentally ill/disturbed (definition is a person who has been hospitalized more than one time);

(g) homosexuals (unless you are homosexual);

(h) unemployed adults;

(i) employers or your teacher or professor or any other inherently unequal relation;

(j) people more than 10 years from your age;

(k) people who need to travel a lot for work purposes;

(l) people who would stop loving you if you were poorer or less physically attractive.

(m) a staunch republican.

14. When is the best time to gauge the sexual chemistry

in a serious relationship?
>   (a) Immediately after the first sexual encounter;
>   (b) Immediately after the tenth sexual encounter;
>   (c) Immediately after the seven-month mark;
>   (d) Immediately after the one-year mark.

15. Which of the following reflects the wisest attitude about sex?
>   (a) Sex is a pleasurable act which should be indulged in for pleasure and to communicate a great liking for another;
>   (b) Sex out of wedlock is a mortal sin that will result in damnation;
>   (c) Sex is a gift which should be used to reward emotional commitment;
>   (d) Sex is a biological drive, like hunger, which should be indulged when the need arises.

16. Which of the following life directives is the most important:
>   (a) Don't engage in wife swapping or open relationships;
>   (b) If you have an affair (a sexual encounter while outside your primary relationship), don't tell your partner;
>   (c) Don't have sex without birth control (unless you want children now);
>   (d) Don't have sex when very drunk, tired, sick, or depressed.
>   (e) Don't have sex just to prove you are liberal or to win acceptance or love.
>   (f) Don't have sex with your boss, your teachers, or any fellow employee who you'll have to see regularly.

17. Which of the following is true:
>   (a) Borrowing money from relatives is the safest and wisest way to fund a new business;
>   (b) Entering into partnerships with relatives is the

safest and wisest way to start a new business;

   (c) Loans relating to a new business should always be clear and written;

   (d) Partnership agreements should be oral because they must be based on trust.

   18. Which of the following is not an important skill that should be learned even if not required in school?

   (a) As early as possible in your education, learn how to touch type on a computer keyboard.

   (b) As early as possible in your education, learn all the basic functions and tools in a word processing program.

   (c) As early as possible, learn basic carpentry skills;

   (d) Learn how to take a photograph with your phone if it has that function.

   (e) By 16 years old, a child should have learned how to use the internet to send and receive emails, including how to send documents as attachments, how to scan documents, and how to download and store documents.

   (f) Learn how to do some basic cooking. You should know enough about cooking to prepare several breakfast dishes (including eggs), several lunch dishes, and at least three different dinner dishes.

   (g) Take a course in public speaking.

   19. Assume you are 53 years old and hold investments as follows: 60% of your cash is invested in a new pharmaceutical company that is applying for FDA approval of a promising new anti-cancer drug, and you are already in the black based on the current stock price; 20% of your cash is invested in rental property that runs a positive cash flow; 10% of your cash is invested evenly in several blue chip companies traded on the New York Stock Exchange; and 10% of your money is in cash and cash equivalents (like treasury certificates). What should you do now?

   (a) Increase your investment in the pharmaceutical company, using your cash, and then sell the pharmaceutical stock after FDA approval;

(b) Decrease the pharmaceutical investment and use the proceeds to increase your allotment to Blue Chips and cash equivalents;

(c) Decrease the Blue-Chip investments and invest more in rental property;

(d) Liquidate the real estate investment and buy the pharmaceutical stock;

(e) Keep these investments as-is, without any changes

20. Which of the following is the correct course of action?

(a) Do not have children until you are married and have been living with your spouse for at least two years.

(b) Have 3 or more children and/or continue to have children until you have one male and female child.

(c) Do not make the decision to have children dependent upon whether you have a steady residence or a steady job.

(d) Do not wait to have children until both you and your spouse are clearly ready. (Don't let your concerns and ambivalence delay your having a child early in adulthood.)

21. Which of the following is bad advice?

(a) Expect that you and your spouse will differ at times about child rearing decisions. Attempt to resolve these inevitable disputes by slow, calm, non-criticizing conversation. Do not quote relatives to support your beliefs.

(b) Child rearing (feedings, changing, etc., etc.) should be divided between two working spouses in proportion to the spouses' incomes.

(c) Treat all advice from relatives (especially grandmothers) and friends as mere recommendations. Do not let anyone give you orders about how to raise your children.

(d) Don't live through your children. Don't demand that they be something you wanted to be or accomplish something that you failed to accomplish. Encourage them to develop their own goals.

(e) Don't give your children severe punishments in the heat of anger. Likewise, don't threaten punishments you won't or can't carry out. Rather, have a calm, fair, reliable set of punishments that you've set in your mind in advance.

(f) None of the above. They are all good advice and life directives.

22. Regarding divorce, which life directive below reflects the wisest course of action?

(a) Don't use demands for money, support, child custody, etc. as a means of punishing your spouse, venting anger, expiating guilt or stopping the divorce.

(b) If you have children, then you must meet and decide how you are going to announce the divorce, and you must announce the divorce together; that is, both parents present and all children present. Neither parent should blame the other parent or encourage the child to take sides in the divorce.

(c) A parent should never leave suddenly without talking to his children.

(d) Once separation has occurred, each partner should carry out their obligations, i.e., facilitating visitation (flexibly), paying child support, etc., exactly on time, without games or power struggles.

(e) When children are involved, neither parent should ever make a promise that is not kept.

(f) Tell all your children, in no uncertain terms, that the divorce is not their fault. In your silence, they will often assume they are in some manner responsible.

(g) All of the above reflect good advice.

23. Which of the following is true regarding education?

(a) Go to school (college) to discover yourself or to find an occupation rather than going with a specific career objective in mind.

(b) At college or university, major in the one of the following subjects: history, English, art, sociology, music, political science, or ethnic studies, to get a good general education.

(c) At college pursue two different areas of study and study them intensely (e.g., computer science and journalism), making sure one of your majors is quite practical in terms of job possibilities.

(d) Struggle to go to a private college with a good reputation, even if it requires that you borrow the necessary funds.

(e) Try to distribute your hard and difficult course work in college such that your most difficult course work is in your final year.

24. Regarding your legal affairs, which of the following is good advice?

(a) Avoid hiring lawyers to do minor legal tasks like evictions, small suits, and divorces. Try to read up and do these yourself (unless very large sums of money are involved).

(b) Don't break the law unless you are certain that your violation will go undetected and unpunished.

(c) If you are charged with a crime and are innocent, waive your Miranda right to remain silent, and answer all questions posed by law enforcement officers;

(d) When hiring a lawyer, search for someone who is older and already famous

(e) Do not resolve (settle) civil actions (suits) out of Court for less money than you want or deserve.

25. Which of the following is false, or bad advice?

(a) If you are a victim of a crime; report the crime

and cooperate with the investigation and prosecution. Women, this especially goes for rape and other sex crimes.

(b) When hiring a lawyer to do a complex task, make sure you hire someone who is a partner at a prestigious law firm with a national reputation.

(c) Don't support propositions to change the law unless you have carefully analyzed the pros and cons, being especially careful about supporting new laws when they are introduced in response to some single case or episode or some current emotional issue.

(d) Don't take the law into your own hands and try to personally produce justice. Solve your problems with people by using the legal process rather than through your own action.

(e) Calmly threatening to file a lawsuit, or better, having an attorney send a letter to this effect, often produces wonders for very little money.

(f) One of the most frequent mistakes people make in their legal affairs is failing to create written agreements when dealing in business and personal financial transactions.

2 WISDOM I.Q. - SCORING

The correct answers are below. Please note that different point totals are awarded for each question based on the importance of the issue. Some answer patterns get bonus points, and some answers can cause point loss. Keep a running total of your points and then look up your Wisdom IQ [WQ] on the table below:

WISDOM I.Q. SCORE TABLE

- 40 POINTS   Wisdom IQ = 130
-
- 35-39 POINTS   Wisdom IQ = 115
-
- 30-34 POINTS   Wisdom IQ = 100
-
- 25-29 POINTS   Wisdom IQ = 90
-
- 20-24 POINTS   Wisdom IQ = 70
-
- Below 20   Wisdom IQ = 50

ANSWERS

1. The answer is "d" (Consider both the short-term and long-term consequences in terms of pleasure and pain, and try to strike a balance insuring some pleasure now with good chances for pleasure in the long run).

This is not a difficult question to answer correctly in the abstract. But it is a master principle of wisdom. Accordingly, give yourself two points for a correct answer; add a two-point bonus if you can honestly say you actually follow this advice for all important decisions; give yourself a one-point bonus if you usually follow this advice.

2. The answer is "a" (Make Love Not War).

The key to this question is reversibility. Tattoos are almost irreversible, and accordingly, the choice is very important. This means that the decision must be made after considerable thought with a focus on how the choice will be viewed many years from now. "I Love John" probably will prove to be very embarrassing when that relationship ends (as most early relationships do). Similarly, "Legalize Marijuana Now" may become outdated by actual legalization, or a change in our understanding of the medical impact of smoking cannabis. "Make Love Not War" is the least offensive, socially, and not likely to become outdated given the lust for violence by modern man.

Give yourself 1 point for the correct answer. Give yourself an additional 1-point bonus if your first response was to resist answering because you understand that no one should get a tattoo given that its limited aesthetic function is outweighed by its irreversibility.

3. The answer is "b" (When to have your first child.)

Having a child, at any time, is an irreversible and profound event. It transforms your life more than almost any other decision you can make. Once made, it cannot be undone. The timing of that decision will control your psychic and financial resource allocations for the next 18 years. Your early choice of your college major, or investments, while potentially very important, are all reversible with relative ease. In the grand scheme of things, your choice of cars, while irreversible in the short run, is ultimately reversible in the long run and trifling in its life consequences.

Give yourself 1 point for the correct answer. Give yourself an additional 1-point bonus if this answer was immediately obvious.

4. The answer is "b" (After two years of college, or age 21 if you do not attend college).

Occupational choice is a CLD (critical life decision). In light of the plethora of occupational choices, it is very unlikely that you would have sufficient information in high school to make an informed choice. Choosing later in life, at age 30 or 35, creates the problem that your entry into the occupational arena, which may require training, will be too late to maximize your chances of advancement and to avoid wasting economic resources on irrelevant educational efforts. After several years of college, or at age 21, you have time to train and make entry while having significant information about the choices and your inclinations and capacities. Of course, your "final" choice may not turn out to be final because you must remain flexible and adaptive to a changing occupational market place.

Give yourself 2 points for the correct answer.

5. The answer is "b" (Get a B.A. degree).

Professionals, like psychologists, lawyers, and physicians usually make good livings, placing them in the middle, upper middle, and lower upper class; but rarely do they become really rich. Even when they have their own practice, they function essentially as employees, i.e., people paid to do work. Real wealth typically arises from owning a business that produces a product, or a service done by someone other than the owner. A general education achieved through a B.A. degree will give you the entry chances you need, while allowing you to enter the arena at a young age. Youth is essential because you will need to experience many failures before you achieve success. The MBA degree is a second-best alternative. The degree does not give you the knowledge, leadership, and creativity needed to create a business; it provides technical knowledge that helps run existing enterprises.

Give yourself 2 points if you answered "b", and 1 point if you answered "f".

6. The answer is "f" (plastic surgeon).

Failure is endemic and painful in all these activities, except surgeon, even if you are very talented. You must be in the 99.9th percentile of competitors and have a character of steal to survive as an artist, actor, or athlete. In contrast, however difficult, there is a high degree of success amongst intelligent hard-working surgeons even when they are not the very "best."

Give yourself 1 point if you answered "f".

7. The answer is "b" (Quietly find another job and then quit)

When you are unappreciated, the work is boring, and working conditions are emotionally damaging, it is rare that things will improve enough to warrant staying on the job. Immediately quitting is unwise because it risks financial hardship if work is hard to get, and it places you in a poor bargaining position when you find a prospective job. (A hungry man is not discriminating when it comes to his next meal.) Immediately quitting is only appropriate if working conditions truly are medically threatening and intolerable. Finally, learning to tolerate painful circumstances is almost always unwise because it erodes self-esteem and long-term health. Generally, denigrating employees and supervisors is an impotent strategy that undermines your own credibility

and trustworthiness when done on a consistent basis.
Give yourself 1 point if you answered "b".

8. The answer is "a" (Take a course in retail sales, skills and techniques)

Underwater welding is a highly technical well-paying job undertaken by very few. It is physically demanding. When you are working in an arena that is highly-specialized, or dependent on robust health, you are at risk, in a changing commercial environment, for being unemployed and defunct. It is imperative that you have alternate job skills that protect you from unexpected changes in the work environment. While taking an advanced welding course may increase your pay, it does not protect you and preserve flexibility. Other courses, which are essentially entertainment, are simply a waste of time until you have handled your over-specialization.

Give yourself 1 point if you answered "a". Subtract 1 point if you chose to sue your employer for age discrimination.

9. The answer is "d" (Take the more regular employment and live with lower compensation.)

These kinds of odd hours, through cycle disruption, cause mild sleep deprivation, i.e., losing two or three hours of sleep a day. When it continues for weeks and months, this schedule can have equally powerful effects as complete sleep deprivation over shorter periods. Chronic mild sleep deprivation, however, is more insidious and dangerous because its effects are less well-known and less obvious. Chronic mild sleep deprivation has the potential to erode relationships, undermine school or work performance, and, importantly, interfere with critical life decisions. The avoidance of complete sleep deprivation and chronic mild sleep deprivation is an important LGD for preserving the minimum conditions of high-functioning and emotional wellbeing. The price that will be exacted for underestimating the importance of sleep can be very high indeed.

Give yourself 1 point if you answered "d".

10. The answer is (e) (the new lesion ignored is the most dangerous), and second most important is (b) (riding on a motorcycle).

The new lesion could be a melanoma, which if left untreated is almost always fatal. Riding a motorcycle as a passenger or rider creates a high risk of serious injury including spinal cord injury causing life-long paralysis.

Give yourself 5 points if you got both, in the right order; give yourself 4 points if you got both in the wrong order; give yourself 2 points if you got one, in any order, and subtract 1 point if you got neither.

11. The answer is "c" (Having regular physical exams and health maintenance screenings after age 40)

All of the choices, except cannabis avoidance, will probably make some small contribution to a long life. But only regular health screening will detect diseases like diabetes, heart disease, and high blood pressure, which can be avoided by early treatment.

Give yourself 1 point if you answered "c".

12. The answer is "c" (Eat four to five small meals a day rather than two or three larger meals)

Give yourself 1 point if you answered "c".

13. The answer is "m" (a staunch republican).

Give yourself 2 points if you answered "m".

14. The answer is "b" (Immediately after the tenth sexual encounter)

Time is too precious to waste many months or a year on any issue that is important to a relationship. On the other hand, making a judgment on a single encounter, or a few, can be very misleading.

Give yourself 2 points if you answered "b".

15. The answer is "a" (Sex is a pleasurable act which should be indulged in for pleasure and to communicate a great liking for another)

Regard sex as a special pleasurable act, like a great movie, play, meal or concert which should be indulged in both for pleasure and to communicate a great attraction and liking of another person. Disregard all views of sex that involve ideas of sin, wrongfulness or dirt.

Give yourself 1 point if you answered "a". Give yourself a 1-point bonus if you laughed when you read choice "c".

16. The answer is "c" (Don't have sex without birth control)

All of choices reflect sound advice, on average. Birth control, however, is the most important because an unwanted pregnancy reliably has a profound impact on life that cannot be reversed.

Give yourself 2 points if you answered "c".

17. The answer is (c)

Give yourself 2 points if you answered "c".

18. The answer is (c) (As early as possible, learn basic carpentry skills)

Give yourself 1 point if you answered "c".

19. The answer is "b" (Decrease the pharmaceutical investment and use the proceeds to increase your allotment to Blue Chips and cash equivalents)

The key principle here is you need to decrease your risk profile as you get older, and avoid investments that can be difficult to liquidate, like real estate. The Blue Chips are safer, because they are not new companies, and they provide some diversification. The current investment in real estate also helps diversification and provides some cash that can be used at retirement. After age 50, having the majority of your investments in a single start-up company is a recipe for disaster. This would make more sense at age 30.

Give yourself 4 points if you answered "b". Subtract 2 points if you chose "a".

20. The answer is (a) (Do not have children until you are married and have been living with your spouse for at least two years.)

Give yourself 4 points if you answered "a".

21. The answer is (b) (Child rearing should be divided between two working spouses in proportion to the spouses' incomes.)

Give yourself 1 point if you answered "b".

22. The answer is (g) (All of the above reflect good advice.)

Give yourself 2 points if you answered "g".

23. The answer is (c) (At college, pursue two different areas of study, and study them intensely, making sure one of your majors is quite practical in terms of job possibilities.)

Give yourself 1 point if you answered "c".

24. The answer is (a) (Avoid hiring lawyers to do minor legal tasks like evictions, small suits, and divorces.)

Give yourself 2 points if you answered "a".

25. The answer is (b) (When hiring a lawyer to do a complex task, make sure you hire someone who is a partner at a prestigious law firm with a national reputation.)

Give yourself 1 point if you answered "b".

3 INTRODUCTION

As we move through time and our lives, we make decisions and plans. Some of these decisions are explicit and conscious; others are implicit in our behavior and conduct. These decisions and plans have consequences in terms of our life satisfaction (Of course, they also have consequences for the lives that touch us). Some of these consequences are immediate and obvious; others manifest themselves more remotely in time, and still others make themselves felt in the deep future. Balancing the proximate and distal consequences of our life choices is the great problem of life. I will offer some suggestions on this dilemma.

I must confess at the outset that I have no special qualifications for giving advice, and indeed, it is doubtful that there are any authentic credentials for the giving of advice. While it is true that I am, by training, a psychologist and attorney, I was never explicitly trained to give advice. Indeed, believe it or not, during the eleven years of college and two post-doctoral years of training that it took to become a licensed professional, I did not take a single course in advice or general wisdom. The reason for this is simple enough—no such course was ever offered. Actually, as you may know, if you have partaken in the occidental version of personally dispensed wisdom, psychotherapists are generally discouraged from giving advice. Just try asking a psychoanalyst for a little advice! You may spend the next year trying to understand what ever possessed you to ask. A little hyperbole here, but a good segue for my first piece of advice: When you have a subtle point to make—exaggerate. While legal training, in contrast to psychological training, does have a focus on "right answers" or "correct analysis," it does not prepare counselors to give advice on anything but narrowest of legal decisions. For example, family attorneys are well trained to know how to advise a client on whether they can prevail on a claim for custody. They are, however, ill-equipped to know whether it is wise to assert the claim. While an attorney can advise you on how to successfully exclude a child from your estate plan, they have no training on how to give guidance on the moral, psychological, and social implications of the exclusion.

One needn't concern themselves with my lack of qualifications and experience relating to life advice because the risk of being exposed to erroneous advice is relatively small in light of the common tendency for people to reject any advice that is not consistent with their own inner wisdom. In fact, if you're anything like me, you often don't even accept and act on your own wisdom. However, if you are one of those rare people who can and do accept advice, let me suggest that you don't allow the advice in this book to direct your behavior unless the advice seems reasonable to you. Of course, in reality, I really don't mean what I say here, because like all people who give advice, no matter what I say to the contrary, I secretly believe that I know best. I "show my cards" here in response to the wisdom: "Don't take people for fools; They'll appreciate that."

Why a book on advice? Basically, there are two reasons for such a text which go hand-in-hand. First, and most importantly, people do foolish things in life which cause them a great deal of misery. Interestingly enough, this maxim appears to be as true for the very intelligent and well-educated person as for the less intelligent and poorly educated person. Second, there does not appear to be, in the common lay literature, any simple, straightforward, and condensed collection of advice on the general issues of living. I do not mean to imply that life is devoid of sources of advice. This is clearly not true. Priests, monks, political activists, palmists, astrologers, professors, financial planners, philosophers, authors, psychologists, psychiatrists, social workers, parents, grandparents, sports heroes, friends, newspaper columnists, and numerous others are all available to some degree, for some limited purposes, at some time for the giving of counsel. It is the very plethora of advice givers that constitutes the problem. The reasonable rules for living must be pieced together in a haphazard happenstance way. And most importantly, they all give their advice too late. Truly useful advice should be deeply settled in the caverns of the mind awaiting the proper moment of life to be activated and called to arms against pending decisional doom. In sum, in the domain of counsel-giving, we don't have good preventative medicine. A problem with the many sources of wisdom enumerated above is that one must accept with that wisdom a great deal of rhetorical garbage. This is especially true of religion which embeds its injunctions and instruction amidst a morass of ideological trappings. The result: One usually suffers from overwhelming distraction or confusion before getting to the core instruction.

This brings to mind the single most devastating quality of advice and advisors—that is, the enterprise of life instruction is, for the most part, reactive rather than proactive. Counsel is sought when things have already gone wrong. Indeed, counseling usually is sought for the purpose of correcting a past failure to be wise. That is, counseling is the bandage solution to a wisdomless culture. Further, once the advisee has, through therapy or some other mode, figured out a way to ameliorate the pains of foolicians (foolish decisions), he or she jumps back into life no better for the process. Ah!! But no sooner do I write this sentence than I hear the therapist's rebuttal: "Good therapy (read in advice, counsel, instruction, astral reading, etc., etc.) teaches lessons that are carried back into the life process. This is the old growth through pain and analysis metaphor. This rebuttal is a good one if life is so gracious as to re-present you with a problem in the domain in which you happened to have learned a lesson. Life is not so gracious. The solution is to get an overview of advice long in advance, i.e., to get a feeling for the gestalt.

Before you conclude that I am obviously taking on an impossible task and that it's unlikely that the advisory content of this volume is any more accurate, if as accurate, as other sources of guidance, keep in mind that the value of this small work does not rest just in its accuracy.

Ultimately, the purpose of this book is to inspire you to look at life in terms of decisional rules. I refer to these rules as Life Guidance Directives (LGDs). It is the discovery of good LGDs that will make you happy. If one of the LGDs discussed in this text doesn't work for you, i.e., if you see it fail in your life or another's, I presume that you'll question and change the rule. What is most important is that life and its vicissitudes be constantly translated and abstracted into useful lessons. This approach will insure the early development of empirically—that is experientially—sound wisdoms. Stated a little more formally: If you experience or witness an unpleasant event which is destructive to you and you wish had never happened, ask yourself what rule of life (LGDs) could have prevented or reduced the likelihood of that event (try to generate a very simple and practical rule).

I share this advice now because I consider this approach the progenitor of all wisdom. This is the principle that inspired this book. That is, all of my recommendations arise out of an application of this LGD. But because this book is going to be incomplete, you must understand this meta-advice—the big daddy progenitor of wisdom. Its application, however, is slightly more complex than it appears.

First, once the noxious event occurs, you must generate not one, but many competing possible rules that would have prevented that event. Now, having these competing alternatives in mind, you must choose which rule is the best rule. Eliminate from your list any rules that are practically impossible. After doing this you must actively look for disadvantages, i.e. problems that will result from following each of the remaining LGDs. Pick the one that has the least problems. Finally, you must compare this new life guidance directive to the results of doing nothing (that is, compare its disadvantages to the noxious event you're avoiding). If your new rule compares favorably, mention it to someone whom you respect (and who appears fairly happy) and see if they can see any problems with it. If not, you've got yourself a temporary LGD, some wisdom. While time and experience may command some modifications of your LGD, you will have some interim guidance. At first, this process is slow and cumbersome. But after a while, it will become fairly easy.

When people try to generate their own life rules, however, they often make errors in three specific parts of this sequence. One common error is to impetuously conclude something from an experience—a rule or imperative—without generating a list of alternatives (a good long list). Second, people often do not think of the potential problems their new rule will itself generate. For example, as a therapist I've encountered a large number of people who, after suffering greatly from rejection by an intimate, have concluded that life would be better if they never got close to anyone. These people are often in treatment for the results of this new rule, i.e. loneliness, depression, emptiness, and conflicting heterosexual (or homosexual) relationships. You may have to live many years with your personal philosophy, so take a little time to think clearly about it.

Finally, people have difficulty understanding and using the concept of relative risk. The concept of relative risk is one of the most essential analytic tools in understanding the potential disadvantages of particular life choices or life guidance directives. While the basic idea of relative risk is simple, it is not understood intuitively or naturally. Relative risk requires an appreciation of chance or probabilities. When doing an analysis of relative risk, you must first compare the risk of some unpleasant event (or some disadvantage) under one set of circumstances against the risk under a different set of circumstance. For example, let us say the risk of getting lung cancer if you don't smoke is one in one million. That is, one person out of a million non-smokers will get lung cancer. Additionally, let us say the risk of getting lung cancer if you do smoke is one-hundred in one-million (i.e., one in ten-thousand). That is, one person out of ten-thousand smokers will get lung cancer. In this example, there are two fascinating conclusions. First, if you smoke, you will be one hundred times more likely to die of lung cancer. Second, even if you do smoke, it is still very unlikely you'll get lung cancer because only one smoker in a ten-thousand gets lung cancer. This does not end the analysis of relative risk. In fully appreciating relative risks, you must also understand generally what the risk is of the adverse event, cancer, under other circumstances. Only then can you understand the relative amount of risk. For example, how would it affect your sense of risk and the wisdom of smoking if you knew that living near the center of Los Angeles, with its pollutants, creates a two-hundred in one-million risk of lung cancer. That is, out of a million centrally located Los Angeles residents, two-hundred will get lung cancer. Accepting these contrived numbers, smoking suddenly seems a bit less dangerous. The idea here is that danger, or disadvantage, must be viewed in terms of probability or risk, and that risk must be viewed relatively, that is in comparison to other circumstances and life choices that create the same kind of risk.

Unfortunately, there are no books that list the risks associated with various life decisions. Accordingly, the concept of relative risk must be used in a murky guesswork manner, where one's sense of risk must often be expressed in terms like, "high," "very low," etc., etc. Notwithstanding these difficulties, the concept of relative risk is still very important. The concept can be applied to any life decision. While I have emphasized its application to adverse events, it is equally applicable to positive events and consequences. For example, imagine that you are eighteen years-old and have been accepted to both Harvard and the University of California at Berkley. You are struggling with whether to go deeply in debt in order to go to Harvard, the school with the better reputation and cache. You know both schools are very good. Your life goal is to be a millionaire before age twenty-five. (A silly goal, but if facilitates our analysis.) So how much more likely is it that you'll become a millionaire if you attend Harvard rather than the University of California at Berkley? Finally, if Harvard does increase the relative risk, or probability, of being a millionaire, does the amount of the increase justify the expense? Of course, no one has the exact answer to these questions. Nevertheless, your estimate or intuition about the answer will be important to your decision. You might conclude, for example, that the cache of Harvard will only determine your initial post-graduation job offers, and that attending Harvard will not provide you with the energy, creativity, and risk tolerance to become a successful businessperson. You might further reason that no one becomes a millionaire from being an employee, and accordingly, in the final analysis Harvard is not going to advance your objectives very much. This analysis, however, might yield a very different conclusion if your life objective was to be socially prominent or to get accepted to a prestigious law school.

In the final analysis, understanding the idea of relative risk will help you keep a focus on how important a particular choice, life pathway, or directive really is for you given your objectives.

Dr. Rex Julian Beaber

4 COMMON SENSE

Common sense is not common. That is, it is not frequently found in ordinary people. Common sense really does not arise from any direct sensory experience. What is common about common sense is that it arises from our common experience, not a body of highly esoteric or technical knowledge. The "sense" in "common sense" is that it is sensible. That is, it is not based on complex logic; rather, it is a product of observing the consequences of decisions in terms of the resulting pleasure and pain. Common sense is pragmatic, not theoretical or philosophical, and it includes, albeit often intuitively, the idea of relative risk. Historically, in the very beginnings of civilization, common sense may have been the only trustworthy source of life guidance. It was soon replaced with religion, superstition, pseudo-science, and tradition. As mankind advanced, true science and technology replaced much of the credibility of religion, superstition, and tradition. In large measure during recent times, common sense has been relegated to the lowly position of a default approach to life decisions when tradition, religion, and science provide no guidance.

What often passes as common sense is, in fact, merely

tradition. The distinction between common sense and tradition is thought and contemplation. Common sense reflects the impact of contemplation on acquired experience. Some traditions do embody common sense because they arose from someone's historical application of common sense. Other traditions are a product of religious guidance or a historical wisdom which has no current application. If one is guided by tradition, rather than LGDs arising from common sense, they are essentially taking a path of passivity in life. In the long run, passivity is almost always harshly punished in the real world.

Happiness is the product of taking an active, or proactive, approach in forming your personal future. Oddly, notwithstanding the adaptive value of actively choosing your life's direction, there seems to be an almost universal preference for passivity. Indeed, the majority of people do not even conceive of themselves as having a myriad of critical decisions in their own life. The experience of acknowledging and experiencing real choice seems overwhelming, and accordingly, many elect to reconstruct their experience such that, moment to moment, they feel like they are simply doing what they must do or have to do. Most people construct a prison of "have-tos." "I have to do this, and I have to do that, and therefore I also have to…." This have-to deductive process is unconscious and reflexive, and ultimately, life destroying. Some of these have-tos are trivial. "I have to go to the market before I go home." Some are momentous and profound in terms of their influence on life events. "I have to get married and have children." Not surprisingly, this distinction between trivial and profound issues marks one of the central tenants in developing critical life directives.

But what is it that allows us to recognize common sense or life wisdom. The answer lies in the application of the pleasure principal. Happiness is achieved when one has optimized the pleasure they derive from life. The pleasure principal acknowledges that one must always view and balance pleasure, measuring both the long and short-term consequences of a life choice.

For example, let us take a high school student having to choose between going to bed early before taking the SAT and going to a late-night party where there will be many attractive opposite-sex participants and lots of fun planned. It is not difficult to see that if your goal were to maximize pleasure in the moment, the party is where you're going. A possible consequence to this choice, however, is the following sequence of events: The student's score on the SAT is significantly lowered; The student is rejected from the best colleges; The student ultimately graduates from a lesser college; The student loses out on the better job opportunities because of his lower credentials; The student makes less income and enjoys a less successful career; The student, as a result, is less happy. This fictional scenario, involving many assumptions and possibilities, suggests that the pursuit of immediate pleasure may, in the long run, actually produce a large net reduction in pleasure.

This analysis, of course, would lead to very different conclusions if the student was planning a career as an artist or professional athlete, where the quality of his or her education may not be an important ingredient of success. Alternatively, if the test was not the SAT, but rather a minor quiz, yet another outcome would arise from the analysis. Indeed, there are always a myriad of uncertainties in this kind of thinking. Maybe the party will result in a police raid and a terrifying arrest. Maybe the student, having under-performed on the SAT, ends up going to an easier college with lessened competition, thereby performs superbly, and with his new heightened self-esteem achieves more after college.

Utilizing the pleasure principal, i.e. attempting to strike a reasoned balance between immediate and delayed pleasure, may not be an exacting science, but it is still crucial to achieving happiness.

As you view your life, you may discover your personal

tendencies and natural biases in applying the pleasure principal. Some people are prone to be governed by immediate gratification. They often are underachievers and have to live with the unpleasant consequences of their controlling impulses. But, they do have fun. Others unrelentingly focus on the future consequences of their choices. They become experts at delaying gratification, and more importantly, they become experts at seeing and exaggerating every hidden risk in immediate pleasure. These impulse-controllers often are overachievers and live lives barren of fun. For them, the future—when the net pleasure could be taken—never comes because they are busy planning yet another future. Understanding your own biases will facilitate your keeping a wiser balance in managing the timing of gratification. It the end, it is balance that produces happiness.

Dr. Rex Julian Beaber

5 CRITICAL LIFE DECISIONS

If all decisions about life were on an equal footing in terms of their impact on life satisfaction, then the task of constructing Life Guidance Directives (LGDs) would be daunting indeed. Obviously, life choices are not equivalent in importance. This being said, it is not always obvious which decisions will prove most significant in any given person's life. Many a fictional drama, and many real lives, have proven that some utterly trifling choice, like running or not running to catch the next subway, can have dramatic life altering impacts—or indeed, can determine if you will continue to live. Notwithstanding Einstein's counsel that "God does not play dice with the Universe," chance events, like accidents, do change lives. We cannot surrender to this factor of uncertainty by withdrawing from the task of constructing LGDs. Instead, we must simply live with the understanding that however carefully constructed, LGDs cannot be perfect guarantees of life satisfaction.

A critical life decision (CLD) is a decision or directive, which will have a large and enduring impact on your life satisfaction. It is imperative that one develop an early sense of the CLDs. CLDs play an essential role in implementing a principle in formulating LGDs. The more critical a CLD, the more time and resources must be orchestrated in developing your LGD. This is a law of human consciousness conservation. Those who fail to appreciate this law, which I call the Rule of Proportionality, are destined to be enslaved by useless obsessive thinking. More importantly, those who fail to obey this law will inevitably fail to establish essential rules of life satisfaction. This is the underlying wisdom that dictates the "common sense" that you must see the forest for the trees.

How do you recognize CLDs? There are some very simple questions that lead reliably to the identification of critical life decisions. First, you must determine if the decision is reversible. More exactly, you need to determine how reversible the decision is and how difficult or costly (in terms of consequences) it will be to reverse the decision. The easier it is to undo a decision, the less likely it is to be a CLD. To cite a very controversial example: The decision to abort a pregnancy, once implemented, is absolutely irreversible. Accordingly, under the reversibility factor, abortion is a CLD. In stark contrast, your choice of major during your first year of college is typically quite easy to change, and the change usually has tolerable consequences. Under the reversibility factor, your college major, at least in the first year, does not look like a CLD. Obviously, reversibility is on a continuum. It is not all or nothing. For example, a marriage can be terminated, but the emotional, psychological, social, and financial costs to reversing your marital status are very considerable.

Second, you must determine if the life choice will have an enduring impact. Typically, your menu selection on a Saturday night date will impact your gastrointestinal well-being for only a few hours. Alternatively, joining the Marines will have life-altering consequences for years. The adoption of a child can have lifetime consequences. The more enduring the impact, the more likely it is that you are dealing with a CLD.

Finally, and most difficult, you must determine if the life

choice will have a large impact on an area of life directly related to your happiness; i.e., you must determine the happiness impact. Your choice of mate (marriage partner or co-habitant) is clearly a choice that will have a tremendous impact on life satisfaction. On the other hand, your choice about which painting to buy to decorate your living room is not likely to have a large impact on your happiness. CLDs are life pathways that will significantly impact happiness over an extended time and which are difficult to reverse. The greater the impact on happiness, the more important the CLD.

The happiness impact factor, however, is difficult to assess because many people do not fully appreciate what really makes them happy or unhappy. Confusion between what is socially expected to produce life satisfaction and what really produces it is one of the most common sources of life-pathway errors. A large percentage of the population invests incredible effort to acquire life situations that will not make them happy. Additionally, enormous energies are wasted on decisions that are not CLDs, while actual CLDs are ignored or treated as already determined. In part, this misallocation of consciousness arises from the fact that trivial decisions are easier to manage, and they give one an artificial sense of control over life.

While there is some individuality in determining CLDs, there are also common life choices that almost universally meet the CLD test. Your choice concerning occupation (or the means by which you will survive financially), your management of money, your mate or marital partner, whether and when to have children, where you live geographically, and certain health habits will profoundly control your life satisfaction. If, for these CLDs, you make sound choices, you have conferred a powerful resistance to adversity and will have created a foundation for true pleasure. Indeed, these CLDs are so important that they can even confer a resistance to bad choices in other arenas. Alternatively, a poor choice in any one of these areas can be

so devastating in terms of its impact that happiness becomes almost impossible. In fact, you will discover that the importance of most decisions ultimately rests on their consequences in these few CLD arenas. Thus, for example, many of your educational choices will be significant only insofar as they are really components or instrumentalities of your occupational choice. In this sense, occupational choice is the primary CLD, while educational choices are secondary CLDs
.

Dr. Rex Julian Beaber

6 THE TEMPORAL PERSPECTIVE

Your remaining time in this life grows shorter each moment, and from a subjective point of view, the rate of aging and the journey to death accelerates as time passes. This painful truth is exacerbated by the truism that your initial allotment of time in this life is very limited, especially when viewed from a grand cosmic perspective of time. Two-hundred years from now, a twinkle in the history of time, your remains will be unrecognizable dust.

If the brevity of our lives were manifestly apparent at its outset, the impact would be emotionally devastating, and, indeed, a complete understanding of the ephemeral nature of existence would exercise a corrosive and undermining influence over every aspect of human endeavor. Fortunately or unfortunately, most of us become aware of the imminence of non-existence only at that point where the disabilities of aging encourage us to welcome death.

Some aspects of brief life are profoundly uncertain and bewildering. On the other hand, there are a number of life issues that appear to be quite certain.

The nature and purpose of life and death, for example, are uncertain and mysterious. That does not mean people are without firm conviction on these subjects. This certainty of belief, however, is in no way a product of clear proof and undeniable experience. Accordingly, it comes as no surprise that throughout time and geography, amongst the many different races and creeds, there are a multitude of different beliefs and convictions on the nature and purpose of life and death. Likewise, it comes as no surprise that the major determinant of your fundamental beliefs about life is simply who your parents are and where you were born.

Other matters are quite certain and appear to be without any doubt amongst everyone but the insane, the mentally disabled, and those who are incurably philosophical. For example, it appears virtually certain that we will all die and that our journey throughout life will take approximately seventy-five years, plus or minus a little based on chance, heredity, lifestyle, and medical intervention. Maybe you will be one of those exceptional people who live a bit past 100; maybe you will die of some dreadful disease, homicide, or accident in early childhood. It is virtually certain that you will not live beyond the age of 130. Accordingly, in a matter of a few hundred years, a mere spec of time, there will not be a single person on the planet who will have personal a recollection of you.

While it would be a cause of considerable misery to contemplate the temporal perspective too much, it would be a cause of even more misery to ignore the imminence of death. Only by remaining cognizant of the brevity of life can you stay focused on the importance of making wise choices, especially with regards to choices that create obligations that are enduring. It has been said that the only thing that you cannot buy is time. While this may be overstated, it is clear that time is amongst the most valuable commodities we deal with during our lives. As we age, this commodity becomes more and more valuable. At age 25, the waste of 5 years of your life in an endeavor that yields little satisfaction, may be a waste of 10% of your remaining life span. At age 70, the same waste will disable almost 100% of the balance of your life. It is for this reason that passivity is one of the greatest of life sins, and it is for this reason that the aggressive adoption and implementation of life guidance directives cannot be abandoned at any cost.

7 WORK, SUCCESS, AND ACHIEVEMENT

"Work is not a curse; it is the prerogative of intelligence, the only means to manhood, and the measure of civilization. Savages do not work"—Calvin Coolidge.

One's choice of work is a CLD of the highest magnitude. Typically, a person spends more than a third of their day working or preparing for work (education). This may be a conservative estimate in a modern society where preparation for the working day, i.e., dressing and traveling, can involve substantial time. Ordinarily, a person will work most of their entire lifetime, i.e. until they are about sixty-five-years old. That is, for a period of about forty-five to fifty-five years, half of all waking hours are devoted to work related tasks and demands. Furthermore, because one's vocation determines in large measure their wealth and self-esteem, work exercises a profound impact on the quality of the remaining half of the day, and indeed, the quality of life after retirement.

Finally, while there is certainly some plasticity in vocational choice, it is extremely difficult to make changes in vocation after the age of thirty-five, and indeed, for many occupational choices, it is quite difficult to do so after age twenty-five. While there may be factors in life that have a greater impact on life satisfaction, e.g. health, work is unique in that its impact is great, and yet it involves a fair amount of freedom of choice. In contrast, you can't choose many aspects of your health status. Your genetic predisposition to suffer from cancer or heart disease or the presence of congenital disorders like schizophrenia or diabetes have immense life satisfaction impacts but are largely (not completely) outside of one's control. Paradoxically, vocational choice is often made very early in life with little appreciation of its significance and with little meaningful information about how one's life will be impacted by the choice. Indeed, children and young adolescents are encouraged to voice occupational aspirations long before they have any idea about the remarkable scope of occupational possibilities in the modern world. Consequently, one of the most important CLDs in our lives is made under circumstances where misguided and ill-informed choices are quite likely.

In light of the dramatic importance of work choice and the highly varied kinds of work that are offered in the modern world, it is helpful to appreciate certain guiding principles in dealing with this CLD. Reward Potential, Reward Likelihood, Work Pleasure, Effort and Stress, Capacity or Skill Demand, Work Hierarchy, and Plasticity are the central factors that must be weighed and balanced in considering work alternatives. These are discussed briefly below:

Reward Potential

A truly rich man makes money while he sleeps. Reward potential is a euphemism for money, or money equivalents. It refers to the highest level of compensation you can receive and your determination of whether this level of compensation is consistent with your "needs" or objectives. For example, if you aspire to be relatively wealthy, then the reward potential from being a dental assistant will probably be too small. Even the highest paid dental assistant cannot become wealthy based on their occupational compensation. Conversely, if you're the kind of person who does not need to be wealthy, then being a school teacher, for example, where maximum income is limited, might be sufficiently rewarding to sustain high levels of life satisfaction. For those who need to truly be rich, the occupational choices are fewer indeed. The reward potential for a business owner, e.g. the owner of rental property, a manufacturing business, or a food franchise, can easily be hundreds of thousands of dollars a year. The potential income of a rock star, professional athlete, or investment banker, for example, can be millions of dollars a year. The factor of Reward Potential focuses on the potential rewards—not the usual reward. Obviously, if your desired income is not within the potential rewards, the occupational choice under consideration will be problematic.

In order to understand Reward Potential, you need good information about the actual compensation achieved within a given occupation, and you need good information about your own "needs" and desires. This information is more difficult to acquire than many realize. There are a myriad of technical vocations that have surprisingly high potential rewards that are not generally known. Understanding your own "needs" or desires can be equally difficult to ascertain.

Reward Likelihood

Reward Likelihood refers to the probability that you will actually reach the reward potential or some particular level of acceptable compensation for a particular vocation. For example, the likelihood that you will achieve the reward potential for the professions of concert pianist, rock star, actor, entrepreneur, or athlete is very very small. Very few people, even amongst those with extraordinary talent, succeed in having any significant income in these and many other vocations. In contrast, a very high percentage of engineers, plumbers, electricians, dentists, teachers, pharmacists, accountants, attorneys, secretaries, and physicians attain the reward potential of these vocations.

Understanding Reward Potential is important because you need to govern your vocational choice based on your tolerance for risk and assaults on your self-esteem. If you have high self-esteem that can resist the pressures of many failures and obstacles, and if you can tolerate a very real risk of ultimate failure, then you can seriously consider the vocations with a low reward likelihood. If you are risk averse and have a fragile self-esteem, then at all costs you must avoid occupations with low reward likelihood. Inattention to your own need for security and the reward potential of your work can be a major source of stress and unhappiness throughout life.

Work, Pleasure, Effort and Stress

Work is the calculated struggle for victory of needs, desires, will, and a plan over the ubiquitous forces of disinclination and laziness. They don't call it work for nothing. Very few people find an occupation that they enjoy doing all day long. People are paid to work because it wouldn't get done if an incentive were not offered. Even those who get a great deal of satisfaction from their work typically find at least some portions of their work demands to be unpleasant. If you set as a goal to discover a line of work that is always pleasant, you should prepare yourself for poverty now. Nevertheless, different kinds of work will generate pleasure for different people. In order to understand the potential for pleasure or pain in a vocation, you must understand what a person really does in the vocation throughout the day. Movies, TV, and parents often provide very distorted or idealized conceptions of what the actual workday is like. Every attempt should be made to talk with someone in your prospective occupation in an effort to gain a realistic sense of the day-to-day tasks that comprise the vocation.

In thinking about work pleasure, you will want to pay special attention to certain sub-factors. First, you should determine how social the work is and your own need for people-contact. If you are a "people person" and have a strong need for, and skills at, social interaction, then certain jobs will be painfully asocial. Accountants, computer programmers, night guards, and certain engineers, for example, lead very isolated work lives. This isolation may be a positive factor for some and a negative factor for others. Jobs in the arena of sales and management, for example, place strong emphasis on social interaction. Second, you should determine how stressful the work is, and importantly, your tolerance for stress. Stress in work arises essentially from time pressure (deadlines) and high levels of expectation. For example, litigation paralegals, the specialists who help trial attorneys prepare their cases, often work under critical deadlines and have their work reviewed often. Some people thrive on these demands. Others suffer every moment under such a work regime. A salesperson in an established posh clothing store, however, will operate under minimal stress. Third, you must determine how physically hard the work is and how willing you are to work hard. Construction work is often quite hard. Physically, computer animation is relatively easy. Many people enjoy physical work and find it more satisfying than social or mental work. Again, understanding yourself is critical. Fourth, you must determine how much problem solving and creativity is required in the work and how this fits with your enjoyment of problem solving and creativity. Movie directors, writers, research scientists, and high-level businesspersons and entrepreneurs, for example, are problem solvers. If you like repetitive predictable work, however, these vocations will be unpleasant. Interestingly, there are some highly compensated forms of work that are very repetitive in their actual daily application. For example, within a few years of graduating dental school or specializing in some kinds of orthopedic surgery, the work is actually very repetitive. Finally, you must consider your interest in the subject matter of the work. Obviously, you are not going to enjoy being a high school English teacher if you don't like English and/or teaching. Blessed is he who has found his work; let him ask no other blessedness. He has a work, a life-purpose, and he has found it and will follow it.

Capacity or Skill Demand

It should be obvious that you must choose a vocation that has a demand for skill that is within your personal capacities. At the extremes, it is not difficult to know if your capacities match the skill demands for a given vocational calling. Concert pianist, mathematician, and world class athlete are vocations that require such rare and extraordinary skills that you can know easily if these activities are within your reach. They probably are not within your reach even if you are very good. Alternatively, receptionist, janitor, and store clerk are vocations that require so little skill that most people certainly could perform the required tasks without much effort. Between these extremes, matching skill-demand and capacity can be more challenging. It is important, however, that the match be close. If the task demands of a vocation are so difficult for you that you must constantly be functioning at your best and working your hardest, then the stress level of the occupation will make it too unpleasant to be survivable for a lifetime. Likewise, if the task demands are too easy, boredom will make the work intolerable. The key is to find a forum for work that is challenging, yet easy enough that you will experience significant success without becoming obsessed with work.

Work Hierarchy

Work Hierarchy refers to your power and independence in the working environment. Relatively early in life, people develop a preference for the level of power or control they need in a working environment. At one extreme, there are those that enjoy working in an environment where their activities are closely monitored and controlled by others, i.e., supervisors or "the boss." Such people enjoy pleasing a "superior" and feel uncomfortable when they have to be self-directing. At the other extreme, there are those that cannot take direction, advice, or control from anyone. Between these extremes, of course, is a continuum of the independence allowed a worker in the work environment. If you need to be independent and in control, it may be best for you not to be an employee. You may need to direct your life towards starting your own business or functioning as an independent professional. If other factors dictate that you will be an employee rather than an employer, and you have a need for control, you will have to structure your life such that you have the credentials and experience to rapidly elevate yourself into management. It is not crucial, however, to be in management to avoid unpleasant supervision. For example, cable TV installers who work in the field often function quite independently during the day after receiving their initial assignments. Because a mismatch between the work hierarchy and your own need for control can lead to real misery, it is imperative that you get a sense for your need for independence as soon as possible.

Plasticity

Plasticity refers to the ease with which you can move from one type of job to another kind of work. Essentially, this refers to how specialized the work demands tend to be. High levels of plasticity are a positive attribute of a vocation. For example, if you train to be an underwater welder doing ship and oil-rig repair and maintenance, you will be working in a vocation with very low plasticity. That is, if for some reason you cannot continue this work, the skill you have acquired will not be very helpful in other kinds of work. Alternatively, in any job where the primary entry qualification is a B.A. degree, plasticity will be fairly high because there are many different kinds of work where a general degree is an important qualification. Generally, you should avoid vocations with low plasticity unless the compensation or other factors are sufficient to offset the risk of unemployability if the work ceases to be available.

Success and Achievement

Modern culture places a tremendous value on success and personal achievement. It is difficult to avoid this influence, and accordingly, almost everyone seeks to actually succeed or to possess the symbols of success within some domain. Whether one seeks the Nobel prize or to be the best pool player amongst his friends, one way or another, everyone seeks success.

While the drive for success is basically healthy, it can become pathologically self-destructive if it takes over one's life. Happiness requires accomplishing a modicum of success that is balanced against the need for more immediate pleasures. As you get older, you should increase your emphasis on pleasure. The arduous foundations for success should be laid in youth and young adulthood.

Success at work, or anything else for that matter, depends on many factors. Nevertheless, there are a few techniques that account for the lion's share of success.

First, it is really true that the longest journey begins with a single step. Unfortunately, it is difficult to take that step if it appears trivial in light of the journey to be completed. For this reason, one of key ingredients to success is to set up a final goal, and most importantly, a series of sub-goals short of the final remote goal, which can be achieved in a realistic time-period, i.e. before you become disheartened with the journey or bored. A plan of attack is an imperative component of a stratagem for success. Thomas Edison once noted, "I never did anything worth doing by accident, nor did any of my inventions come by accident; they came by work."

There is a master principle of planning that is very helpful to achieving success. This principle is backward planning. Think about your final goal, and then think about what would have to be accomplished just before you reach the goal. Think about the last step. Then ask yourself, "What would I have to accomplish just before that, and just before that, etc., etc., until you are at the beginning of the process. Interestingly, this is also a master principle of problem solving (Try going backward in a maze problem. You will be delighted with how easy it becomes). It is very important that both the final goal and the sub-goals or interim goals be realistic. A realistic goal is one that is within your capacity to reach using ordinary efforts. If your goals require that you function at your limits for long periods of time, the level of stress and the risk of failure make the effort unwise. There are more victims of unrealistic goals than of chance misfortunes, and accordingly, wise goal-setting is a key to happiness.

A second step in producing success is setting up personal rewards (self-reinforcement) which you provide yourself upon completion of sub-goals. The ability of self-reward is a central characteristic of the successful. Self-reinforcements can include rest from the struggle, food, entertainment, trips, purchases of special items, etc. Self-reinforcements help produce success, and they create balance in life. A balance between work and struggle, on the one hand, and pleasure and reward, on the other, is an important component to life satisfaction. Continuously postponing pleasure weakens or paralyzes the pleasure response and creates the risk, in the case of goal failure, that pleasure is not achieved. Alternatively, postponing work and struggle insures that future pleasure will be limited.

A third step is persistence and hard work. Edison taught that his invention of the lightbulb was ten percent inspiration and ninety percent perspiration. This is universally true for those who succeed. Most failures overvalue their great ideas and underestimate the importance of persistence in the face of frustration and failure. Almost every successful person failed many times before succeeding. Learn to expect and tolerate failure. Learn to use failure as a time for assessment and re-evaluation, not self-deprecation. Having said this, it is also important to be able to give-up. Some ideas sound good and are bad. Some ideas can't be accomplished for practical reasons beyond your control. Sometimes you do not have the talent to succeed. Sometimes the effort, pain, and social cost of going forward is just not worth it. You must be able to give-up because only then can you go on to the next good idea. Finding the balance between persistence and having the flexibility to relent is one of the difficult tasks for which there is no sage wisdom. But, you must consider the choice.

Finally, it is important to escape from social approval as your driving force in setting goals, sub-goals, and an allowance for pleasure. We live in a world where parents, friends, movies, the internet, TV, and the popular press directly or implicitly set up the desired goals for the general population. Unfortunately, many internalize these goals with little real thought about whether the goal, if achieved, will actually produce life satisfaction. The result can be a life filled with a desperate struggle to achieve an outcome that has no fulfillment potential. Life is too short for this kind of mistake. At some point, it is imperative that one stop and really ask what they want and what makes them happy. There are, for example, millions of people who have internalized the model of spouse, children, and family as a core life goal when in fact this lifestyle will not produce a pleasant life for them. Once the choices are made consistent with this goal, i.e. marriage and children, the result may be irreversible consequences that impact virtually every other life decision.

Advice on Work

1. Work and work accomplishments no matter how hard or trivial give meaning, direction, and joy to life, so you should always work. Never retire; obliterate fantasies about not working (which is a bore), and focus on making your work hours as pleasant as possible (Note: raising children, doing the yard, etc., etc. are all work).

2. Make your work goals realistic and well within your limits; don't stretch your limits to please others or to meet societal norms.

3. Keep your work life from overly dominating your home life; keep a good perspective about the importance of your work. Your major love interest should be first and your work second.

4. You should develop some broad occupational skills (or develop two sets of separate skills) so that changes in the marketplace or economy do not leave you stranded. Along similar lines, even when secure in a job, keep abreast of alternatives and don't burn bridges, e.g. alienate significant persons who may later be instrumental to other work.

5. Regardless of your pay or the goodness or badness or your boss or conditions of employment, struggle to meet a high standard of skill in your work.

6. Make a decision about what kind of work you want to do as early in life as possible; then begin immediately to prepare for that work. Don't wait for the perfect work; leap

into a possibility now.

7. If you dislike your work, do not complain or allow yourself the luxury of depression; rather, look for alternate work or learn a new skill. Never substitute complaining for a problem-solving action.

8. Don't quit a job unless you have an alternate job or course of action clearly laid out in advance.

9. Within your area of work, set up little day-to-day and month-to-month challenges around which you can organize your efforts. Keep many of these challenges short-range so that you have many small success experiences.

10. Learn to finish tasks at work. Avoid starting too many little projects. While some tasks have to be done simultaneously, always have some which are begun and finished without interruption.

11. Inevitably, you'll encounter a superior who is wrong, unfair, unjust, incompetent, cruel, insensitive, etc. Understand that this is inevitable and that you do not have to confront such people with their faults. With a person who has power over you, try once or twice to calmly and unthreateningly reason with them; should this fail, either quit or quietly succumb; don't waste your energies on long-term battles.

12. If you have a number of jobs competing for your attention, do the most difficult one first.

13. When choosing your future life work, take into consideration how much money you will earn and decide if you will be comfortable with the lifestyle it provides.

14. When making a career choice, take into consideration how hard you want to work to get your degree, etc., and how many hours you want to work once you're there. Be realistic. You know yourself best.

15. Project yourself ten or fifteen years into the future on the job. Fantasize about the day-to-day requirements and payoffs. Are these thoughts comfortable, exciting, or unpleasant? These fantasies should give you some clue as to whether or not you really want this career choice. Better,

find a person who has this job and talk with them about what it's like on a day-to-day basis.

16. Don't be afraid to make social ties with the people you work with. Here you can find some very valuable and rewarding friendships. After all, they have something in common with you, the basis of all good friendships.

17. Dress appropriately for the job, and watch your posture, gait, etc. People will judge you by these things.

18. Have a desk and area at home where you can sit down and take care of your personal affairs and any business you do at home (bills, phone calls, reports, studying, reading journals, etc.) It's important to have a single space designated for work.

19. Do not convey deeply personal aspects of your life to people at your workplace unless the person you are talking to is a friend away from the workplace. Further and most importantly, assume that anything that you convey confidentially will be public knowledge within one month.

20. Before you send an email at work or to a fellow worker or supervisor, read it twice. After the first read, ask yourself if you would be comfortable with the email if it was read by every employee and supervisor. Ask yourself, "How this email would look to a future employer." During the second reading, proof the email for spelling, grammar, and word choice. You are going to have to live with this email forever; they don't disappear.

21. Once you set a goal, be persistent and focused. Persistence, in almost all areas of human accomplishment, is more important than intelligence, natural talent, or any other factor in determining success. Some failure or setbacks is a natural process of all significant endeavors. Respond to failure and setbacks by attending to the cause (not blaming) and thinking of steps to put you back on track. Be open to the possibility that you, or some aspect of your approach, is the basis of a setback. Use this conclusion to plan the next step—not self-depreciation. Focus, which involves thinking exclusively at critical times

about your goal and the steps it will take to accomplish your goal, is second only to persistence.

22. Learn to give up and surrender. It is paradoxical that success requires persistence and focus, and yet failure can be produced by an unwillingness to give up on a goal or a plan. Find the dynamic harmony between persistence (which becomes stubborn obsession when pursued blindly) and flexibility (which becomes pathological meandering when adopted too quickly). Persistence should be your default; flexible development of new methods or goals should be adopted only when repeated persistence fails and your analysis of the cause of the failure indicates that factors beyond your control, and unlikely to change, are the basis of failure. Many lives are ruined by a refusal to face reality and formulate new goals.

23. Do not criticize or verbally denigrate a boss, supervisor, or fellow employee. Avoid the language of personality (e.g. "Jason is an egotist."), and use the language of behavioral analysis (e.g. "It is difficult to increase my sales when Jason refuses to refer customers to our department."). Do not lie about your boss, supervisor, or employee.

24. Do not criticize or verbally denigrate your own employees when you are talking to a fellow supervisor or employee. Avoid the language of personality (e.g. "Jason couldn't sell matches to an Eskimo."), and use the language of behavioral analysis (e.g. "Jason's sales remain below expectation despite repeated efforts to show him better sales techniques.").

25. Employers and supervisors should make a concerted effort to find verbal and non-verbal ways to reward employees on a regular basis. Genuine verbal praise and recognition is a very powerful instrument for incentivizing a work force. Do not give verbal praise when criticizing some aspect of performance or when you are asking an employee to do more work. Give sincere undiluted praise at least once a month. Small non-verbal rewards (e.g. "you can take off today at noon") are powerful motivators.

26. Listen carefully to your employees, and solicit their views often, because many times a low-level employee, even one with minimal training or experience, may have profound observations about the workplace and productivity. Do not underestimate employees based on position, education, training, gender, or their introverted style.

27. Employers and supervisors should never threaten to terminate an employee unless they really intend to follow through and have a clear reason to do so based on performance or legitimate business needs. Employees should not quit or threaten to quit unless they mean it and can afford the economic consequences. Generally, employees should not quit unless they have another job in hand.

28. Employees should have a habit of arriving and leaving work on-time without excuses or lies. Similarly, they should work hard and not repeatedly take sick days when not actually sick. Employees should agree, under special circumstances that occur rarely, to work harder than usual and for longer hours, without seeking additional compensation. Workers should not agree to work longer hours or extra days without additional compensation when it becomes a regular pattern.

29. Employees should avoid being ingratiating or overly friendly with bosses and supervisors. A little psychological distance between employees and supervisors is important. Employees should avoid counting on a single supervisor to protect them against adversity or unfairness. They should cultivate a friendly respectful relationship with at least two "superiors."

30. Ask for help when you need it. Do not be embarrassed to ask for help.

31. Do not have a sexual, romantic, or business relationship with anyone at work who has substantial more or less power than you in the work environment. (Here, business relationship refers to a business outside the work

environment.) Do not borrow from or lend money to coworkers.

32. With the exceptions noted below, you should avoid entering into the following occupations as a primary manner of earning a living: professional musician, artist, actor, rock star, athlete, politician, gambler, and any other profession where failure and rejection is a regular consequence for the majority of those attempting to earn a living in such an occupation, even those of exceptional talent. This advice should be ignored only by those who are objectively the best of the best (nationally) and who have such high self-esteem that they can tolerate years of failure and disappointment.

33. Develop skills and training, during your life, in at least two occupations.

8 SLEEP

When you think of it, it is quite amazing how much time we spend asleep. At birth, and for some time thereafter, it is not uncommon to sleep eighteen or more hours a day—more than 75% (three fourths) of the day! By old age, our time at deep rest comes closer to 25% (one fourth) of the day. This is still a staggering amount of time. Over a lifetime, people will spend approximately 33% (one third) of their lives in the state of sleep. That is, during a seventy-five-year lifetime, twenty-five years will be spent asleep and unconscious! This is truly incredible. Sleep is either a consummate waste of valuable time or it has a value that is rarely acknowledged.

Sleep is to the brain as food is to the stomach. Sleep is an essential element to brain health, and like food, even short periods of deprivation can have a dramatic impact on mental well-being. Complete sleep deprivation for a day or two can lead to emotional volatility, angry outbursts, confusion, and poor judgment—including potentially life-threatening poor judgments. Sometimes, when sleep deprivation goes beyond three days, it can lead to complete mental disorganization and psychosis. In contrast, a similar period of food deprivation would have far fewer deleterious effects.

Importantly, mild sleep deprivation, like losing two or three hours of sleep a day, when it continues for weeks and months can have equally powerful effects as complete sleep deprivation over shorter periods. Chronic mild sleep deprivation, however, is more insidious and dangerous because its effects are less well-known and less obvious. Chronic mild sleep deprivation has the potential to erode relationships, undermine school or work performance, and importantly, interfere with critical life decisions. The avoidance of complete sleep deprivation and chronic mild sleep deprivation is an important LGD for preserving the minimum conditions of high functioning and emotional well-being. The price that will be exacted for underestimating the importance of sleep can be very high indeed.

Like food, sleep is largely a matter of ritual and habit, and it is a part of the daily cycle. The sleep cycle, however, is also delicate, and it can be disrupted easily. The delicacy of the sleep cycle increases as you get older, and accordingly, being attentive to preserving the sleep cycle through sleep rituals becomes quite important as we get older. That being said, the establishment of your sleep cycle begins very early in life and can have significant consequences for achievement and life satisfaction. For example, the cycle of sleep where you are an "early riser" appears to confer certain life-long advantages in the area of achievement. This follows from the fact that many life activities, e.g. school, the opening of the stock market, traffic, etc., etc. are time-linked. It is also true that the cycle of sleep controls the cycle of daily energy. There are individual differences in the need for rest, i.e. the number of hours of sleep required to achieve rest, and there are also differences in preferred cycle, i.e. bedtime. Early sleep habits, however, are a strong determinant of preferred sleep cycle. Most importantly, preferred sleep cycle can be modified early in life. Choosing and implementing a productive sleep cycle may not be CLD, but it may be quite important.

Sleep, however, seems to consist of something more than mere rest. About a quarter of the time we spend sleeping is spent dreaming. Reality is a multi-act play. Dreams are multiple one act plays. Ah, the paradox of dreams: The only time my mind is truly free, yet my body is in prison. Ah, the wisdom of sleep! While it is well-understood that dreaming is essential to mental health, much else about the subject matter remains hotly debated. Certainly, you could go a lifetime ignoring your dreams and still have a good and happy life. Nevertheless, some attention to dreams and their potential meaning may heighten the enjoyment of life and may enrich your experience. It takes little effort to reflect and think about dreams, and as long as it does not become obsessive, there is little risk of harm. Regardless of the true meaning of dreams, if there is any meaning at all, contemplation about dreams can lead to some creative thoughts about your life and your current struggles. Accordingly, creating the environment for sufficient sleep, and for some free time to enjoy dreams, facilitates optimizing life enjoyment.

Advice on Sleep

1. Pattern your life so that as an adult, between the ages of twenty-one and forty, you sleep between seven and nine hours a day. Avoid sleeping more or less than this amount for any sustained period.

2. Pattern your life so that as an adult between the ages of forty and fifty-five, you sleep between six and eight hours a day. Avoid sleeping more or less than this amount for any sustained period.

2. Avoid sleep deprivation. Avoid going with less than five hours of sleep for more than two days in a row.

3. Males: Don't sleep more than 9 hours a day. Females: Don't sleep more than 10 hours a day (Exception: days when you are compensating for a period of sleep

deprivation).

4. When you are ill, sleep as much as you can.

5. Sleep on a firm mattress. Don't try to save money on a cheap mattress. Remember, you spend a third of your life in bed.

6. Go to bed early and get an extra half-hour's worth of sleep before an especially challenging day, e.g. a final exam or a special presentation.

7. Sleep in a room that gets some fresh air, e.g. open the window just a crack.

8. When asleep, either wear no clothes or loose-fitting clothes.

9. If you have trouble sleeping, do the following (try combinations of these):

(a) Get up and read or watch T.V. until you really get tired (or do some other work around the house). Don't lie in bed awake.

(b) Determine if you are worrying about something and see if you can get up and solve or plan to solve it.

(c) Eat something (especially try warm milk).

(d) Take a warm shower or bath.

(e) Increase (or decrease) the room temperature.

(f) Stop drinking coffee, tea, cola, and alcohol within four hours of bedtime.

10. Don't ever take drugs to get to sleep unless it is an absolute emergency or unless you are suffering from a medically-diagnosed depression.

11. If you have dreams that you don't like, plan to have a dream the next day and plan to have the dream change in a positive way. Before going to bed the next night, think about your corrective dream and plan how you want it to go. Treat your dreams as something you can partially control.

12. Get in the habit of remembering your dreams and share their contents regularly with a friend or lover. Regard your dreams as a symbolic commentary on your current life. Don't regard your dreams as predictive.

13. Don't smoke in bed. (Under the health section, of course, it is advised that you don't smoke under any condition.)

14. Don't sleep in the same room as your children or parents.

15. Before going to sleep each night, try to solve and communicate about leftover problems with your lover-mate. Don't go to bed angry. Resolve problems before sleeping so that each morning you start fresh. Begin this pattern early in your relationship.

16. Don't make your children go to bed when they are obviously not tired.

17. If you have children between the ages of two and about ten, have a nighttime ritual where you tell them a story with a little lesson and they also tell you a made-up story.

18. Ask your children about their dreams and teach them that they can change their dreams. Talk about dreams at the breakfast table.

19. If you awaken at night with a painful cramp in your calf (lower leg), then grab your foot and pull your foot so that your toes are pointing at your knee (as if you were going to stand on your heels). If this doesn't work, then get up and walk around.

20. Create a ritual around going to bed. Go to bed at about the same time each evening, and prior to entering bed, engage in ritual activities like brushing your teeth, checking lights and doors, etc. Create a package of signals that tell your mind and body that sleep is coming.

21. Structure your life such that you go to bed before eleven P.M—preferably by ten P.M. Wake up at approximately six A.M.

22. If you have no trouble falling asleep but chronically find yourself waking up in the very early morning before you have completed your sleep, then consider the possibility that you are suffering from depression or that you are worried about some unfinished business, or the ambient room temperature is too hot or cold.

23. Keep a flashlight next to your bed in case of emergencies.

24. Make your bed a special sanctuary for rest, sex, and comforting contact. Avoid eating in bed, working in bed, and using the internet or watching TV in bed.

9 HEALTH AND BODILY WELLBEING

"The scorn of death is again one of the methods of prolonging life...The best way not to die too soon is to cultivate the duties of life and the scorn of death"
—Alexander A. Bogomoletz

In part, the amelioration of illness can be purchased, but vibrant health can only be had at the price of sweat and sacrifice. Remember, while your illness may happen to you, your response to that dilemma happens to your illness.

Personal health is a paramount critical life arena. Unlike many other important life arenas, poor health has the capacity to completely nullify the joys and pleasures arising from other life arenas. Indeed, over a short period of time, even a paltry flu with fever, vomiting, muscle aches, and lethargy can totally nullify the immediate joy of riches and a great love. Needless to say, a life-threatening illness like cancer, heart disease, AIDS, etc., can, and usually will, decimate all of life's bounty. In contrast, even poverty does not necessarily make happiness impossible.

Health issues are not only critical because of the magnitude of pain they create; they are also paramount because they are virtually inevitable and difficult, or impossible, to control. One hundred percent of the population will die. Everyone will die; most will become quite sick before they die. Almost no one travels throughout life without encountering a significant episode of illness. Additionally, we are destined also to encounter the insult of health problems in our siblings, parents, and children.

In light of the importance of health issues, it is paradoxical that a high school graduate is more likely to know how to solve problems in geometry than be able to articulate even the most basic knowledge of disease and medical treatment. Typically, the obsession with health information does not arise until late middle age, when health problems are either knocking at the door or well ensconced. In youth, and even young adulthood, feelings of invulnerability and/or the temporal remoteness of death foster a palpable ignorance of the most rudimentary issues in medicine.

No matter how knowledgeable one becomes regarding health issues, and no matter how wealthy one becomes, thereby permitting access to healthcare solutions, death and illness are virtually inevitable, and accordingly, we may never really attain any high degree of control over physical pain and suffering. Despite all the advances in medicine, the maximum life span has changed very little in modern times, and indeed, even the typical life span has only modestly changed. This change is due mostly to the advent of antibiotics and the reduction of infant mortality, relatively old features of modern medicine. Because life is the only game in town, however, we must make some efforts to lengthen life and reduce physical suffering during life.

While the most dramatic increases in well-being come from self-promulgated lifestyle habits that are preventative, the treatment of health problems almost always requires the intervention of a professional. Choosing this professional wisely can be life-saving. The two critical qualities for a health professional are integrity and good training (skill). Ordinary people without special training or experience in health care are prone to judge health care professionals based on their apparent compassion, warmth, interpersonal skills ("He remembers my name!"), and so-called "bedside manner." In fact, these human dimensions have no particular correlation with actual skills, and indeed, they are sometimes adopted as a substitute for careful evaluation and skill. While it is tempting to use interpersonal attractiveness as the primary basis for choosing a physician, it should be avoided. Furthermore, in many modern countries, the level of health care will depend less on the qualities of the physician and more on the economics and organization of health care delivery. In choosing your medical care, one needs to be aware of the economic motives of the system, not just the integrity of individual providers.

Advice on Our Body – Our Health

1. On both your computer and in hard copy, keep copies of all of your health records including reports, evaluations, surgery notes, blood tests, procedure reports, etc. In this regard, be diligent in acquiring these records because they will not be provided to you as a regular practice. In addition, in a separate single document you create, record the following information: Your name, address, phone number, emergency contacts, blood type, serious allergies, each of your diagnoses, your current medications (with dosage), your history of surgeries and hospitalizations, your insurance information (including all numbers and codes necessary for billing), and the name, address, and phone contact for every physician that has treated you. Bring a copy of this information to your first appointment with any health care provider.

2. By age thirty, you should acquire good health insurance. Many will be insured by their employer or through some government mandate, and accordingly, they will have limited choices about the system or the provider. However, if you have a choice, you should avoid health

maintenance organizations (HMOs), and you should avoid insurers who do not allow you to have a wide choice regarding providers. If you do not get insurance from an employer or through government mandate, purchase it even if the cost will interfere with some of your more discretionary expenses.

3. Be an active participant in your health. Use the internet to research every diagnosis you are given and every medication you are prescribed. Use the internet to research any physician that treats you and to search for highly qualified physicians. Do not passively accept referrals or diagnoses without attempting to educate yourself.

4. Make sure your general practitioner schedules you for all routine health screenings including PAP, HPV, HIV, Colonoscopy, Bone Density, and any others that become standard. Similarly, make sure you and your children have all recommended immunizations.

5. Don't drink any alcohol more than two days in a row. Don't drink more than two glasses of wine (or the equivalent in hard liquor or beer) on any given day. If you do not have the self-control to follow this rule, don't drink alcohol.

6. Don't smoke or consume cannabis more than twice a week. Generally, use all intoxicants moderately, and if you can't follow this rule, don't use them at all.

7. Have your teeth professionally cleaned three times a year regardless of whether you think you need cleaning this frequently.

8. Gargle well (for at least one minute on the clock) with hydrogen peroxide (3% solution) once per week.

9. Brush your teeth, gums, and tongue thoroughly at least once every other day, and floss well at least once per week. (Obviously greater frequency would be better, but this minimum will have remarkable preventative power for your dental health.)

10. Unless it is an emergency, never let a dentist extract a tooth, other than an impacted molar, without getting a

second opinion.

11. Do not allow dental problems, e.g. cavity, chipped tooth, etc., to go untreated for more than 30 days.

12. Wear seatbelts, drive calmly and carefully, and never drive within two hours after drinking more than one glass of wine, beer or a shot of whiskey.

13. Weigh yourself (stripped, in the morning) every day on a medical balance scale. Purchase a medical scale (they are expensive). It's a great lifetime investment.

14. Maintain your weight within 20 pounds of your ideal weight (determined by ideal weight-height chart) for your entire life. If you weigh outside this zone of safety, by even one pound, immediately go on diet until you are three pounds inside this zone of safety. Do not postpone losing weight for any reason; do it when you have very little weight to lose.

15. If you suspect you have a medical problem (other than the routine cold or flu) seek medical help immediately. Don't let fear or cost slow you down. Almost every significant health problem is easier to treat at the beginning stages.

16. Early in life, by age twenty-two or twenty-three, designate for yourself a personal physician. Use this physician as a coordinator of your medical care. Be sure this physician is Board Certified in either Family Medicine or Internal Medicine. Choose a physician who is relatively young (under 35).

17. Women should designate for themselves a gynecologist or family physician, and they should see this physician regularly for routine screening and health maintenance including mammograms, PAP, and HPV testing.

18. Don't consent to any non-emergency surgery without seeking an outside opinion from a relevant expert.

19. Don't seek care from chiropractors or other non-physicians until you first consult your personal physician.

20. Don't take medical advice or treatment from friends

or relatives (even if they are physicians).

21. Don't smoke cigarettes. Don't have even one.

22. Do some form of exercise, one that you enjoy, for twenty minutes at least three times per week. Be sure you exert yourself enough to sweat, get your heart beating fast, and feel tired. Additionally, walk casually at least one mile a day, five days a week. Do not engage in obsessive exercising that inflicts painful wear and tear on your muscles and joints. Be moderate in your exercise routine and strive for long-term consistency, not bodily perfection.

23. After age forty, take 1,000 mg. of calcium, two "baby aspirins," and 1,000 I.U. of Vitamin D3 every day.

24. Don't allow your life to be dominated by any theory that says foods can make you healthy or sick. If you exercise regularly and maintain your weight within 20 lbs. of ideal, your diet will make very little difference unless it lacks sufficient variety to insure an array of vitamins and minerals.

25. If you need medical help from a specialist, be sure he is Board Certified in his specialty (this is especially important for plastic surgery, oncology, and cardiology).

26. Don't have plastic surgery to perfect yourself. Use plastic surgery only if you have a severe defect that makes you ugly or interferes with some bodily functions.

27. If you have children, then child proof your house. Place all poisons and small sharp objects out of your child's reach or behind locked cabinets.

28. Don't ever put or have put a tattoo on your body. Never walk into a tattoo parlor while under the influence of alcohol.

29. Never ride a motorcycle (neither as a driver nor as a passenger) regardless of whether or not you use a helmet.

30. Don't engage in dangerous sports like parachuting or other sports where equipment failure can cause death, or where speed, height, or the presence of sharp objects creates risk of serious bodily harm. Don't trade a few moments of excitement for permanent bodily injury.

31. Don't ever have a gun in the house that is not in a

locked cabinet and unloaded.

32. When you go to a physician, prepare a brief and clear list of your current concerns, symptoms and observations, and use this list to ensure that you leave his/her office with all questions answered.

33. Take a shower or bath every day.

34. Men: if you're going to have sex with a prostitute, then use a prophylactic.

35. At around age forty or forty-five, sit down with your wife or some other close relative and discuss with them the issue of death with dignity; spell out whether or not if you were very ill, say with cancer, and were unable to participate in your own medical decisions, whether you'd want your doctors to pursue extraordinary life-saving procedures to keep you alive (e.g., surgeries, resuscitations, life sustaining machines). Share the results of this discussion with your personal physician. Fill out any state authorized forms used to insure your wishes are respected.

36. Make sure your child has a family physician or a pediatrician for the purpose of giving your child routine immunizations.

37. If you discover a lesion (abnormal area) on your skin that is new, dark, has irregular edges, or in any manner creates a suspicion that it could be a melanoma, then see a Board-Certified Dermatologist immediately without delay.

38. All women should learn how to do self-examinations of breast lumps to facilitate early detection of breast cancer.

39. Avoid occupations (jobs) and hobbies where you'll be exposed to asbestos, radiation or chemical fumes.

40. Do not allow yourself to get sun burned, or to suffer exposure to direct sun light for more than 30 minutes a day without good sun protection clothes or medication.

41. Find some method of relaxing yourself for at least a half hour each day. During this half hour, do not work, don't try to accomplish anything, breath slowly and deeply, relax your muscles, and think of pleasant thoughts and

fantasies. Taking a long casual walk at the end of the day works wonders.

42. Unless your physician specifically recommends it, don't take laxatives more than two times per year. In general, avoid non-prescription drugs and especially avoid using them on a frequent, regular basis.

43. The evening before any planned surgery, take one general vitamin, 1,000 mg. of Vitamin C, and eat a meal high in protein and fiber.

44. Attempt to eat some roughage: raw fruit or vegetables, whole grains (in bread or cereals), or bran every day.

45. Don't force your children to eat when they are not hungry.

46. Don't dye or bleach your hair before age 40.

47. If you develop a chronic medical problem, e.g., hypertension (high blood pressure), heart disease, colitis, diabetes, arthritis, etc., go out and buy a book on the topic and learn about the disease, and especially attempt to understand what your role will be in controlling the disease. Use the internet to research the disease and learn about new developments.

48. If you need surgery, hire a surgeon who has done the particular procedure many times.

10 FOOD AND EATING

"The best sauce is hunger"—French Proverb.

From a strictly biological perspective, eating food is simply a method of supplying the body with a source of energy (calories), building parts (fats, protein, and carbohydrates), and chemical facilitators (vitamins etc.). Because food is absolutely essential to survival, the drive to eat (hunger and craving strength) is extremely powerful and resilient, and the pleasure derived from eating is extraordinary. As it turns out, animals, including humans, are quite inefficient, and accordingly, they need to refuel two to six times per day. This would be real drudgery were it not for the pleasure associated with eating and the amazing creativity of humans in fashioning a myriad of variations of taste and texture. In modern societies, the real problem with food is that the potency of all the culinary delights induces us to consume more calories than we actually need to function (We are programmed to store the excess calories as fat as a safeguard against future food scarcity). While at an early point in our species history we might have used thousands of calories a day to hunt down, capture, cook, and eat our protein sources, now we can purchase a year's worth of calories by engaging in essentially verbal legerdemain while seated. The net effect of our "success" at food production, and reducing the physical labor required for survival, is that our caloric storage departments, fat cells, have grown beyond our aesthetic toleration. Managing this issue is crucial to physical wellbeing and social opportunities.

While food is of vital importance to survival, in many ways its importance is exaggerated. Popular folk wisdom and half-science regularly suggests that subtle variations in food intake are responsible for almost every disease, overall life span, physical beauty, youthfulness and mood regulation. In fact, if you manage your food intake, such that, you stay within twenty lbs. of your ideal weight, and you eat a variety of foods from the various groups (fruits, vegetables, grains, fish, meat), you will avoid most food related problems without having to obsess about food theories. The marginal increase in health that comes from following food theories is simply not worth the resulting reduction in the pleasures of eating. Seek balance, not perfection.

Food Advice

1. Eat when you are mildly hungry. Don't eat out of habit when you're not hungry, and don't structure your life such that you fast and then eat when extremely hungry.
2. Don't adopt a vegan diet.
3. Eat four to five small meals a day rather than two or three larger meals.
4. Drink green tea at least once a week. Drink coffee freely but not more than five times per day.
5. Drink at least one full glass of water (clear) per day.
6. After age thirty, drink between two and five glasses of wine per week, but do not drink more than two glasses of wine in any given day. Alternatively, drink an equivalent amount (in terms of alcohol content) of beer or hard liquor.

If you can't follow this rule, don't drink alcohol at all.

7. Females should eat 6 oz. of red meat at least twice per month.

8. Males and females after age thirty should eat at least 6 oz. of salmon at least twice per month.

9. When dieting, consume high levels of protein, low levels of carbohydrates, drink lots of water, and take a general vitamin per day. Take a rest from your diet for one day every two weeks, and plan your diet such that you do not lose more than three pounds per week.

10. After age twenty, eat a dark green vegetable at least three days a week (three meals).

11. Eat a fresh fruit at least three days a week (three meals).

12. Eat slowly and savor your food.

13. Regarding dinner, avoid eating alone, and avoid eating while doing another task.

14. Once a month, splurge and eat what you like without adhering to any rules or diets.

15. Learn to cook or make at least two kinds of breakfast, lunch, and dinner. Don't structure your life such that you need someone else to prepare your food and have no independence.

16. Never attempt to control weight gain by using laxatives or inducing vomiting.

17. Learn the calorie count in your favorite breakfast, lunch, and dinner foods.

11 LOVE, ROMANCE, AND MARRIAGE

The initial part of a relationship is like a private showing of artwork. Sometimes, the artwork is so beautifully framed that one confuses the frame with the quality of the art itself.

The beginning and end of our love relationships will be amongst the most intense and dramatic times in our lives. The potential for euphoria, delirious happiness, titillation, dejection, sadness, and depression is incredible. This range of emotions is a tribute to the social bonding capacity of our species. One of the most crucial aspects of love relationships can be understood by paying attention to the interesting phrase "falling in love." Why the use of the "falling" metaphor? The reason is the universal subconscious awareness that at some point, the process of attraction and bonding is out of our control. With this reality comes love's greatest pleasure and greatest danger. At some level, we covet the opportunity to surrender to a greater force. At another level, it is terrifying because control has always been our lever against psychological pain. There is, however, an important lesson that can be learned from looking more closely at the metaphor of "falling." When standing at the edge of a cliff, before you step or jump off, there is a moment when you can step back and step-away. There is a temporal instant where rationality can dictate your fate, a decisional nodal point. There is a point where you can decide if it is a delightful ocean below, or dangerous rocks. A moment later, after the fatal step, choice is lost and gravity (love) takes on a life of its own. The lesson is that you must exercise your rationality, your self-protective choice, before you take that step that surrenders to love. You do, must, and can choose, at some point, to step back from love. Use this decisional nodal point to protect yourself, and you shall gain access to one of life's greatest joys.

Reminder: As you read the advice below, you may be tempted to respond to any particular directive by thinking that you know people who have violated the directive and had great marriages and mates. Exceptions are not exceptional. If there are a hundred-million long term relationships in the United States, then even if a directive were wrong only one percent of the time, it would mean there are a million exceptions. Accordingly, these directives, like all of the directives in Sage Advisor, are simply calculated to put the "odds" on your side.

Advice on Love, Romance, and Marriage

1. Don't date a man or woman who is living with another woman (man).

2. A woman on a date should take along enough money, in cash, to come home by taxi from anywhere in the city.

3. Don't go out with someone whose conception of the future of your relationship is substantially different than yours. Your goals and intentions should match. Be straightforward in your intent; you'll save a lot of time and pain.

4. Don't engage in any sexual activity that you are not comfortable with, and don't allow yourself to be in a situation where you'll lose your choice in this matter, e.g. his/her house, a mountain top, etc., etc.

5. Don't go out a fourth time with someone whom you

didn't like and enjoy in the first three encounters.

6. Don't continue in a relationship with someone who wants to control the details of your dress, speech, eating behavior, religious beliefs, political beliefs, make-up, etc. Avoid very controlling people. Avoid people who are repeatedly suspicious of your commitment. Seek people who like you as you are.

7. If your intent in dating is to establish a long-term relationship, then date within your socioeconomic class, or at least close to the same socioeconomic class.

8. Assume that another person's faults and imperfections will remain and will not improve, and therefore decide if you can live with those imperfections. If not, discontinue the relationship immediately. Don't try to change adults to conform to your needs and desires.

9. Sexual chemistry is very important in a relationship. If the chemistry is not there by the fifth time you have had intercourse, then it probably won't be there ever; end the relationship.

10. Sex is not a game or a gift. If you care for someone, respect them, and are physically attracted to them, and if they share your intent with regard to the relationship, then have sex and enjoy it.

11. Don't date or marry any of the following:

(a) alcoholic; (b) drug abuser: (c) policeman (unless he works regular hours); (d) medical interns; (e) recently divorced (1 month); (f) mentally ill/disturbed (definition is a person who has been hospitalized more than one time); (g) homosexuals (unless you are homosexual); (h) unemployed adults; (i) employers or your teacher or professor or any other inherently unequal relation; (j) people more or less than eight years from your age; (k) people who need to travel a lot for work purposes; (l) people who would stop loving you if you were poorer or less physically attractive.

12. Don't go out with anyone who insists on keeping any part of their life secret from you.

13. On a date, wear clothes that are consistent with your usual comfortable dress; likewise, women, use your regular make-up.

14. Go out with people who are warm, who appear to want and need physical non-sexual contact. Judge warmth by how they treat others, not you.

15. Don't go out with anyone who is cruel to animals. Don't go out with a man that actively hates his mother, and don't go out with a woman who actively hates her father.

16. Follow the twice and you're out rule. If in the course of a relationship, a person strikes you more than once, terminate the relationship immediately and irrevocably (Many would suggest the rule should be "once and you're out." However, sometimes intense emotions can bring about inappropriate behavior in an otherwise good person). Don't be cajoled into violating this rule by apologies and promises.

17. If, after one month of "dating," your relationship is not clearly intensifying, end it and find another opportunity.

18. Look nice for a date and take care of basic hygiene, teeth, hair and bodily cleanliness. Don't let these degrade over the course of the dating relationship. Don't take your present mate for granted.

19. Use dates as a time to try new fun activities; purposely explore new forms of pleasure and entertainment. Alternate this approach with dates where you go places and do things which you reliably enjoy. This will create a harmonic balance between stability and exploration. Play together and stay together.

20. If you find that your mind is often wandering when your mate is talking, or that you are bored, end the relationship.

21. A date is a joint activity; both persons should share and participate in the planning and costs whenever possible. Your date is not there to entertain you; actively work together and talk about ways to spend your time. Say what you want. It's hard to please a silent partner.

22. If you are dating a person who has had prior serious relationships or marriages, learn what problems ended those relationships, and ask yourself if there are seeds of that problem in your present relationship.

23. Establish preferred patterns of habits you want in a relationship as early as possible.

24. If you like, care, love, etc. a dating partner, tell them in no uncertain terms. If they cannot respond in kind within ten days, get out of the relationship. But if they don't respond in kind, don't let that stop you from telling the next partner your liking, etc. Don't play games with expressing your feelings.

25. Don't go out with someone who is substantially less or more intelligent than you, but don't confuse education with intelligence.

26. It is imperative that you mate with someone that shares an interest in some joint activities other than sex. Sex is very important in a relationship, but it is insufficient to sustain the relationship.

27. Don't go out with a friend's boyfriend or girlfriend without their prior approval.

28. Don't lie to a date unless you don't want to go out with this person again.

29. Plan the time on initial dates such that 60-80% is engaged in clearly planned and structured activity and 20-40% is unstructured and free; increase the free time during the course of dating.

30. Involve yourself with someone that shares your basic values in the areas of religion, politics, child bearing, the importance of wealth, and the geography of your home and work. Explore these issues early in your encounters so that you can avoid falling in love with someone who will be, in the long run, a bad match.

31. You are going to disagree, and you are going to argue. Don't require perfect harmony as a condition for continuing the relationship. But do follow these rules: Don't shout; don't hit; don't blame; don't tell your mate that

they are mentally ill or defective, or otherwise engage in name-calling, and don't interrupt. Do listen and try to understand your mate's view of the disagreement. Do tell your mate what you understand is their position, and make sure that they agree before you describe your position (This is not a suggestion to agree with their position; this is a suggestion that you make sure you understand their position). Do tell your mate the exact behaviors that are the problem (i.e., focus on the behavior not your inferences and conclusions). Do tell your mate how their behavior makes you feel. Do tell your mate exactly what you want in behavioral terms.

32. Don't try to make people love you. Don't struggle to be loved. Don't change yourself to be loved. If they don't love you, end the relationship.

33. Don't marry someone unless you have lived with them for at least six months.

34. Don't get married before the age of twenty-three. It is preferable to get married after age twenty-five.

12 SEX

Sex is that great bodily pleasure that causes neither obesity nor addiction. "Sexual pleasure, wisely used and not abused, may prove the stimulus and liberator of our finest and most exalted activities"—Havelock Ellis

Notwithstanding the social movement toward equality between the sexes, men and women shall probably remain quite different with regards to sexual pleasure. Generally, men are aroused more easily, aroused mostly by visual sexual stimuli, achieve orgasm more quickly, and have less need for a significant relationship before consummating the sexual act. From an evolutionary point of view, men are built, biologically, to disseminate their reproductive seed. Women, alternatively, arouse more slowly, take longer to achieve orgasm, are more aroused by non-physical attributes of their partner, and feel a greater need for the protective cuddle of a warm committed relationship. From an evolutionary point of view, women are built, biologically, to be less impulsive in their mating and to therefore exercise wiser choice about the potential father of their children. Much of the sexual tension in modern relationships arises from these biological forces that are more than a million years old. Accordingly, mutual blame, frustration, and anger aren't justified and do not advance the agenda.

Advice on Sex

1. Regard sex as a special pleasurable act, like a great movie, play, meal or concert which should be indulged in both for pleasure and to communicate a great attraction and liking of another person. Disregard all views of sex that involve ideas of sin, wrongfulness or dirt.

2. Women: Unless you want a child now, take precautions against pregnancy. Do not allow yourself to become pregnant unless you actively choose to do so. Don't wait to take precautions until after you sexualize your relationship. Don't believe anything a man says about his fertility unless you've spoken to his physician, and in general, don't believe anything a man says in the heat of sexual passion.

3. Don't make marriage, total love, or total commitment a condition for having sex. Acknowledge to yourself that it is okay to have sex at different times for different reasons: play, love, warmth, pure hedonism, and to put an end to boredom.

4. Immediately terminate your relationship with any person who ever forces you to have sex or whoever feels a need to hurt you (physically) during a sexual act.

5. Use sexual fantasies to make sex exciting. Don't be afraid of your natural desires to enhance the sexual experience, but don't allow yourself to have fantasies about illegal sexual behavior.

6. Use sexual variety to enhance sex. Oral sex, mutual masturbation, different sexual positions, and different locations (indoors, outdoors), etc. all help. Introduce variations slowly, savoring each, and always leaving something new for the future. Note: Sexual intercourse is over emphasized as the centerpiece of sexual activity. Actually, oral sex and mutual masturbation are more effective sources of pleasure. Pace yourself—you've got a

lifetime to explore.

7. Don't engage in wife swapping or open relationships. If you have an affair (a sexual encounter while outside your primary relationship), don't tell your partner. This new popular form of "honesty" is very destructive.

8. Women: Use self-stimulation, masturbation, as a method of teaching yourself how to have and enjoy orgasm. Start this practice in adolescence.

9. Don't have sex when very drunk, tired, sick, or depressed. Don't have sex just to prove you are liberal or to win the acceptance of love.

10. Don't have sex with your boss, your teachers, or any fellow employee who you'll have to see regularly. If you violate this rule in hopes of a permanent relationship, be prepared to find a new job or a new employee.

11. Women: Don't regard having sex as a bargaining tool or as a weapon. Don't think of it as something men need and you don't want.

12. Men: Remember, women, for anatomical reasons, rarely have orgasms during intercourse. Use oral and manual sex to stimulate orgasm. Pursue sex slowly and attempt to produce (help produce) orgasm in the woman first.

13. Women: Don't make a big deal about losing your virginity. Attempt to have your first sexual experience with an older, experienced lover. Same advice for men.

14. Avoid sex with people who have multiple sexual partners.

15. Allow yourself a brief period in life, one or two years, when you engage in lots of sexual exploration with different partners. Regard this as both fun and good preparation for a positive sexual relationship with your true love.

16. Preserve the specialness of sex by creating a good environment that is attractive. Don't allow sex to become habitual and mundane. Candles, showers, good clothes, scents, a touch of wine, no curlers, clean teeth, etc., etc.

17. One of the great sexual positions is the woman on

top, definitely try this. The woman can get great pleasure if she does the moving in this position.

18. Men and Women: If a lack of natural lubrication in the woman is causing too much friction, with pain, or difficulty with penetration, then use saliva (spit applied during oral sex) or KY jelly (or an equivalent) as lubricants.

19. Men: If you are having trouble with ejaculation too soon, try one, some or all of the following: (a) Masturbate to orgasm several hours before sex; (b) Have sex with the woman on top and let her do most of the moving; (c) Slow down thrusting as you feel orgasm approaching: (d) Stop your more stimulating fantasies as you feel orgasm approaching; restart them as your arousal slows; (e) As you feel orgasm approaching, relax your muscles especially the anus muscle; (f) Use a lubricant to reduce friction; (g) Place your penis deep into the vagina and keep your up and down (in and out motion) short; moving out (up) only an inch. Avoid having the head of the penis move in and out of the vagina. Don't over stimulate the head; (h) Take a very low dose of Viagra, or some equivalent.

20. Women: If you want to increase the chances of orgasm during intercourse, either stimulate yourself by hand, during intercourse, or shift your body forward so that you can cause the shaft of the man's penis to stimulate the upper end of your vagina (the part closest to your stomach).

21. Don't have sex with someone whom you are not sexually attracted to.

22. When having sex, let your partner know when he/she is making you feel good; don't keep your pleasure a secret; your moan can add greatly to the excitement. Excitement is exciting.

23. Don't criticize or laugh at your sex partner during the sex act. Comment on the sex after it is over.

24. During the sex act, communicate warmth and love; never talk about banalities, T.V., work, money, etc.

25. Don't get sexually involved with someone who is presently sexually involved with a friend or relative.

26. Don't "share" private sexual facts, or your comparative evaluation of someone's sexual skills, with anyone but a very best friend or psychotherapist. Abstain from revenge by sexual critique, and respect the privacy of your prior partners. Exception: Do communicate any violent or abusive sexual conduct to anyone in the community that may be a future victim.

27. People do vary in their sexual needs. Nevertheless, when you are younger, i.e., between sixteen and thirty-five, have sex (including both self-stimulation and with a partner), two to four times per week. From thirty-five to forty-five, aim for about one to three times per week; after forty-five, once or twice a week; after sixty, once a week to once every two weeks. While these are only guidelines, you should give some thought to a situation where you substantially depart from these guidelines.

13 FAMILY

As the cell is the unit of life, so the family is the unit of civilization. The family is the only mechanism by which the capacity for love and civility can be passed on to the next generation. As Aristotle noted: "It is characteristic of man that he alone has any sense of good and evil, or just and unjust, and the like, and the association of living things who have this sense makes a family and a state."

Advice on Family

1. Do not have more than three children or less than two children. Do not have any children until you are at least twenty-five, and preferably don't have children until you are thirty. Do not have children if you can't afford to take care of them. Do not have children if you have not completed your education or occupational training.

2. Never allow a family member (sister, brother, mother, father) to live in your home in the first five years of your marriage.

3. Never allow an adult family member to live in your home for an indefinite period. All such arrangements should be the exception, temporary, and with a time limit

set in advance.

4. Once a month (Sundays are great), have a family day where members of your nuclear family (spouse and children) spend a day having fun together. Do this as a ritual.

5. Never attempt to borrow money from relatives, lend money to relatives, go into business with relatives, be partners with a relative, invest with a relative, or purchase property with relatives.

6. Should necessity or emergency require you borrow from or lend money to a relative, have a clear written statement about what will be paid back and when. Avoid gifts and vagueness in these matters.

7. Avoid seeing members of your extended family (mother, grandmother, cousin, etc.) more than once per month, unless you actually enjoy such visits. Avoid visits that are done out of duty. When visits are done for duty reasons, attempt to structure an activity that you may enjoy.

8. In disputes between your spouse/mate and your family or her/his family, side with your spouse...unless you are planning a divorce.

9. Prior to the death of your mother, father, grandmother, and grandfathers, set up a special meeting with each during which time they should tell about your family roots: i.e., the names, birth places, occupations, special talents, etc. of your distant relatives that you could never meet.

10. Treat relatives as potential advisors; seek their opinions and reasoning, but do not communicate the message that you want or are willing to take their direction or directing. Treat them as consultants. Do not reject parental advice just to prove your independence, and don't accept it to prove you're a good son or daughter. Finally, if you accept the advice, present it to your spouse as your idea, and do not use its parental source as a persuasive device.

11. If you hate or dislike a relative or a spouse's relative, then show this feeling by withdrawing from this person.

Don't waste your psychic energy by arguing with them, trying to change them, or talking with others about them.

12. Almost everyone has old and deep resentments (angers) at some family member (especially one's mother or father) for their past behaviors. Handle this by using the on-off system; that is, either forgive them and live in the present, or hate them and cut off relations. Anything in between is destructive.

13. Arrange your life so that in old age, when you may be ill and unable to work, that you can be self-supporting. This will require considerable planning in your late thirties and early forties. Don't destroy your children's adulthood by forcing them to be your caretakers because you did not plan for age-related disability.

14. Grandmothers must avoid criticizing how their daughters raise their children. Grandmothers should even avoid helping their daughters or offering any unrequested advice. Grandmothers should never use the word should. When giving advice, the phrasing, "You might find it helpful to try _____" is the best format.

15. When you encounter family problems, that is problems with your spouse, children, parents or in-laws, seek a consultation with a professional early during the problem. The therapist you seek should be either a licensed clinical social worker, licensed psychologist, or board-certified psychiatrist. He/she should have a family approach and should be inclined to see the whole family, or parts of the family, together in sessions. If your problems persist for more than six months while seeing a therapist, then fire the therapist. Never bring a family problem to a person who does psychoanalysis or insists on doing only individual therapy sessions. Your therapist should appear curious, smart, extroverted, clear-speaking, practical, and fair.

16. Don't compare the accomplishments of one family member to another family member. Avoid ever comparing brothers and sisters.

17. Try to find the unique, positive attributes of family members and use these to praise them during conversations.

18. Many families have a scapegoat, that is, a person everyone agrees to blame and dislike. Don't participate in family gossip and scapegoating; withdraw from these conversations or break the pattern by praising that person.

19. While family is very important, you must have at least two good friends who are not relatives and who are not friends of your relatives. Develop and cultivate these relationships.

20. A biological connection is not always a good reason to be in a relationship. If a family member is psychologically destructive, consider terminating the relationship and seek sustenance elsewhere. You can't make your parents or grandparents love you, and some are not fit to be loved.

14 IMPORTANT SKILLS AND KNOWLEDGE

There is a plethora of skills and morsels of information that would be helpful to daily living that are not automatically taught in the course of regular schooling. Some of these skills can have a profound impact on your life; others are just very helpful and convenient. Many of these skills can be acquired in school, but because they are not required, you will need to make a specific effort to get the training. If your school does not teach these skills, acquire them in the private sector.

Advice on Important Skills and Knowledge

1. As early as possible in your education, learn how to touch type on a computer keyboard. This is often referred to as the QWERTY system. You should be able to effortlessly type thirty words per minute with few errors. True touch-typing requires that you can type without ever looking at the keyboard.

2. As early as possible in your education, learn all of the basic functions and tools in a word processing program.

Currently, WORD and WORDPERFECT are two excellent and widely used programs.

3. Learn how to take a photograph with your phone if it has that function.

4. By ten years old, a child should have learned how to use the internet to send and receive emails, including how to send documents as attachments, how to scan documents, and how to download and store documents.

5. Learn how to do some basic cooking. You should know enough about cooking to prepare several breakfast dishes (including eggs), several lunch dishes, and at least three different dinner dishes. You should learn how to use a stovetop, a microwave, and an oven for basic dishes.

6. Take a course in public speaking. Additionally, join the speech and debate club of your high school or junior high school and regularly participate in their activities. No matter how afraid you are of public speaking, and many do have this fear, take every opportunity early in your life to speak in public to an audience.

7. Learn a technique for remembering people's names when introduced. Practice that technique and adopt the practice of regularly addressing people by name.

8. Study a map of your city of residence and learn the basic geography by heart.

9. Learn how to listen to people very carefully without interrupting or guessing what they are going to say next. This doesn't mean you need to agree. But it is crucial that you fully understand what is being said to you. Don't respond to a lengthy comment about something important without confirming with them that you do correctly understand their view.

10. By age twenty-one take a formal CPR (cardiopulmonary resuscitation) certification class. Also, learn how to do the Heimlich maneuver.

11. Take a course in self-defense. This is especially important for women. Make sure the course is a practical course that prepares you for being assaulted, rather than

training in a formal martial art. (Note: Judo is not useful for these purposes.) Courses in Karate and Jiu-jitsu are useful. A superficial course won't do; It should be at least three months, twice per week.

12. By the age of eight years, you should have learned to swim the length of a thirty-five-foot pool twice without assistants or floats. By age sixteen, you should be able to comfortably swim two-hundred yards without assistance. Parents, it is your responsibility to ensure this is done.

13. By six years old, a parent should have trained their child when and how to call the emergency 9-1-1 number in your city.

14. Regardless of whether you have a car, by age eighteen, you should know how to drive a car. You should also know, by heart, the basics of the subway and/or bus routes in your city.

15. If you do not speak the language spoken by the majority of people living in your city of residence, learn and master that language. If alternatively, you do speak the majority language, but another language is spoken by a significant minority, then get basic skills in the minority language.

Dr. Rex Julian Beaber

15 MONEY AND PERSONAL FINANCE

Money is little more than a device for keeping the record of our productivity. It is a common denominator that we use to exchange our productivity for the productivity of others. Nevertheless, money elicits powerful, albeit divergent, responses from almost everyone. George Bernard Shaw has said, "Lack of money is the root of all evil." While Robert Louis Stevenson shows a compelling disdain for money when he hyperbolically declares, "The price we have to pay for money is paid in liberty." I suspect that Thomas Babington was right when he said, "Even the law of gravitation would be brought into dispute were there a pecuniary interest involved."

Usually, whether we realize it or not, money is typically used to buy some pleasurable sensation. When we spend, we get that sensation soon. When we save and/or invest, we get the pleasure later. Sometimes, the pleasure lasts moments (e.g., ten minutes with a prostitute, or a scoop of Häagen Daz®). Other purchases, like a house, provide pleasures potentially for a lifetime. Often, when considering an expenditure, it is useful to ask exactly what pleasurable sensations you are buying, how intense they are, how they compare to others that could also be purchased, and how long the pleasure will last. Interestingly, the cost of many products and services is in no manner proportional to the relative pleasure derived. Does a $200 bottle of Cabernet Sauvignon really taste ten times better than a $20 bottle? Is the difference anything more than hype and illusion? We are often depleting our personal financial resources on differences without a difference.

Money and monetary value are often very useful in understanding a human conflict. It is often useful to ask, "Could I make this conflict disappear by an expenditure of money?" It is surprising how often money will solve a conflict, and it is even more surprising how little it often takes. It may not be wise to spend the money that it will take to end a person-to-person conflict, but it is almost always helpful to do that evaluation.

Advice on Money

1. Always struggle to save some money, if even a little, on a monthly basis, in case of an unexpected emergency. Do this even if it requires sacrificing some pleasures.

2. Save in order to buy the more expensive better quality, longer lasting item, rather than impulsively buying an inferior product that will need replacing or which you won't like.

3. Don't buy on credit unless the item being purchased is immediately necessary for survival or temporary emergency purposes. Every month, you should pay off the entire balance of your credit cards. If you can't do this, you must spend less and reevaluate how you spend your money. The one major exception to this is the buying of a house.

4. Husbands and wives should have separate checking and savings accounts. They should also have separate credit cards, in their own names.

5. Don't borrow money from friends, fellow employees, and relatives. Pay back all of your debts and obligations promptly.

6. Early in life, a person should develop the following monetary devices: two major credit cards, a checking account, a savings account and a check guarantee card. Early in life, you should learn how to use the bill-paying device available within online banking services.

7. Plan your monthly expenditures by subtracting from your pay, your known expenses (rent, phone, food, utilities, savings, etc.), and then allot the remainder to yourself as a pleasure allowance (for movies, books, etc.). Always buy what you really need first, and then buy what you want or gives you pleasure. Most people have a very distorted view of what they "need." You need much less than you think.

8. If you are divorced and plan to remarry, document what assets you had prior to your new marriage and ask your new spouse to sign an agreement (written by an attorney) that acknowledges that these assets (money and property) are not part of your joint community property. Do this even though it is unromantic.

9. Generally over your lifetime, you should take the greatest risks with your money when you are younger, and you should decrease risks as you get older. After age forty-five, you should be very conservative and risk-averse in your investments and use of money. Prior to age thirty-five, you should make some high-risk investments that may have a very substantial return over the long run.

10. Don't invest money in a business venture that you are not going to run, unless you a) have thoroughly investigated the people involved, and b) and can afford to lose all your money. Treat such investments as a form of gambling.

11. Don't make large purchases and financial decisions impulsively. Take your time. Suspect anyone who rushes you to make purchases or investments as a conman (especially when large amounts of money are involved).

12. Keep a running balance in your checkbook so you always know where you stand.

13. When you use a credit card, immediately subtract

the amount from your checking account, just as if you wrote a check, so that when the bill comes, you can pay it immediately by check without your checking balance suddenly changing.

14. Keep hidden, somewhere in your house, a good sum of money, say $500.00 in cash, in case you have an emergency need for quick cash.

15. In the ash tray of your car, have small change for use in meters, etc.

16. Keep hidden in your car $100.00 in case of an emergency.

17. During early childhood, ages five to eight, give your children a daily small allowance for doing certain special chores (not chores that you require). As your children get a little older, eight to thirteen, give the allowance on a weekly basis. Finally, in adolescence, ages thirteen on, give allowance on a monthly basis. Allowance should be given after work is complete, and older children should buy certain "necessities," (like sports equipment) from this allowance.

18. Children over eighteen who are not in school and who are living at home should make a financial contribution to the house for room and board, or if this is impossible during hard times, they should be required to do work around the house. Several months prior to a young person's leaving home, this contribution should be saved by the parent and given back to the child on leaving to aid in initial expenses (first and last months' rent, etc.).

19. Couples living together without children should attempt to share expenses equally. If one person makes a lot more money, there should be a clear agreement on how to divide expenses and a written agreement on who owns what, especially property, if they separate.

20. Don't buy a house with a lover that you are not married to or do not plan to marry.

21. A woman should not have children until she feels certain she can afford not to work for six months after

childbirth.

22. When buying products, e.g. food, stereos, cars, clothes, etc., pay for real differences in quality or functionality, e.g. taste, lowered future repair costs, durability, etc. Do not pay for fancy trade names or differences that salesmen point out, but which you can't understand, see, feel, or otherwise experience. Don't buy things just because they are popular, the newest fad, or "in." Focus on function not image.

23. Try to own a home or a condominium by age forty. Save carefully to do so.

24. Every once in a while, give yourself permission to make a foolish expenditure.

25. In general, buy things, not services. Attempt to buy objects that hold their value or increase in value. Males especially should avoid spending significant sums on expensive cars designed to impress. These cars don't make you more valuable as a person, and over time, the wasted money will interfere with smart savings and investing. Women should follow the same advice regarding clothes and jewelry.

26. If you have children, then buy some life insurance and name your husband or wife as the beneficiary.

27. Don't brag about your monetary assets; be modest about any wealth you have.

28. Don't marry just for money, but don't be ashamed of your desire to fall in love with someone who makes money.

29. After age forty, you should work diligently at diversifying your portfolio. All of your investments and financial hopes should not be in one investment, or even one type of investment. Divide your investments between cash (or cash equivalents), property, stock (which should be divided amongst different industries), bonds, art, and gold. Put yourself in a position where disruptions in a part of the economy does not decimate your financial security.

30. By age forty, you should have enough saved cash to

support yourself and your family for six months. Don't spend money on pleasures and discretionary items until you have met this goal.

31. Don't delegate your financial, investment, and business affairs to others. Make your own decisions, do your own research, and take personal responsibility for your financial affairs.

32. Many eastern religions and philosophies view nirvana as being achieved by wanting and needing less, i.e. transcending desire. In contrast, western cultures often contend that satori is achieved by producing and having more and satiating every desire. Finding a balance between these two views is the central key to the good life.

33. Generally, with few or no exceptions, the return on an investment in money is directly proportional to the risk of loss. Accordingly, very safe investments, like U.S. Treasury Certificates, have very low but secure yields. On the other hand, purchasing stock in a startup company or some new technology that is not fully developed is very risky, with a real risk of losing all of your money. These risky investments, however, sometimes have very high returns. If anyone tells you about a low-risk "sure thing" investment with a high return, do not make the investment. If this person attempts to rush you into such an investment, assume that they are a conman.

16 FRIENDS

A relative loves you despite your identity—a friend, because of it. Any person with one lover, two friends, healthy children, money, and health is rich; if he doesn't feel that way, he's a fool. Most likely your parents will die within your lifetime. Your lovers or spouse may leave by divorce. Your children, if you have them, will be available but really shouldn't be a major source of support and companionship. In the final analysis, friends may be the most important support system to sustain you during the inevitable trials and tribulations of life. The importance of sustaining a few good friendships over the course of your life simply cannot be overstated. This said, Aristotle's reminder should never be forgotten. "He is his own best friend, and takes delight in privacy, whereas the man of no virtue or ability is his own worst enemy, and is afraid of solitude." —Aristotle: Ethics, IV, 3. Quoted by Durant, The Story of Philosophy

Advice on Friends

1. Cultivate and maintain a close friendship with at least two people at all times during your life. Do not try to be friends with a large number of people, and don't confuse an

acquaintance with a friend.

2. In friendship, follow the rule of equity. Trade evenly all the various commodities of friendship. Return all borrowed money promptly. Be as willing to lend as to borrow. Return phone calls and initiate contacts as frequently as your friend. When meeting, try to be fair and equal about who travels how far to meet. Disclose yourself as much, or a little more, than your friend discloses him/herself to you. Trade equally on little favors, etc., etc.

3. Always listen to your friend. Try desperately to understand his view of the world and of you. Take advantage of your friend to learn honestly how others view you. Don't be angry at your friend for being honest with you about your faults.

4. Don't take advantage of your friends. Don't use your friends.

5. Be loyal to your friends. Don't drop a friend or withdraw from a friend for minor arguments or faults. Don't believe what other people say about your friends until you've told your friend and assessed his explanation. Always give a friend a chance to explain him/herself.

6. Tell the truth about yourself to your friends. Don't try to get your friends to like you for some manufactured image. Let your friends see the real you and take it or leave it. Hold onto these friends who know the foolish, evil, and childish parts of you.

7. Share your plans and thoughts about your future and your goals with your friends. Seek their advice and reflection, but of course, always make the final decision about your life yourself.

8. Don't do anything illegal or immoral (using your moral standards) to impress a friend or to get a friend's approval. Do not be a slave to your need for approval from your friends.

9. Don't let a friend take advantage of you or otherwise perpetuate an unequal relationship. If a friend is maneuvering into a one-up position, then share your

perception with him/her. If this game playing doesn't stop, then end the relationship.

10. Try to have a non-sexual relationship-friendship with a member of the opposite sex throughout your life.

11. Attempt to see your current friends at least twice per month.

12. Arrange a time with your friends so that you have at least a half an hour of unstructured time to spend just relaxing and talking (no sports, TV, or other distractions) each time you are together.

13. Avoid having all your friends in one social class, occupation, or religion. Try to have some variety in your friendships.

14. Do not become romantically involved with a friend's lover, wife, ex-wife, ex-lover, etc.

15. Don't go into business with a friend. If you violate this rule, at least have a clear written agreement with him/her about all the details of the business (especially who does what, who gets how much, and how to handle one person wanting to end or change the business).

16. Don't work for a friend, and don't hire a friend to work for you.

17. Don't be friends with people you know are criminals or alcoholics.

18. Don't be angry with your friends for not taking your advice. Don't make the acceptance of your advice a condition for being in a relationship with you. But do offer your advice and the reasons for your advice to your friends. Don't deprive a friend of your experience or knowledge.

19. When talking about your friends to other people, brag about their positive traits and defend them (when they deserve it) against untrue or unfair attacks.

20. Seek out friends that have some common interest with you (e.g., a sport, hobby, etc.). If you have a friend who doesn't share some fun activity that you can do together, then sit down and see if you can't take up some hobby together.

SAGE ADVISOR

21. If for some reason it becomes necessary to end a friendship, avoid being continuously angry about the friend and trying to get other people to take your side; just withdraw from your friendship; this is your most powerful weapon.

Dr. Rex Julian Beaber

17 BOOKS

Books are the refrigerators and freezers of ideas; keeping good ones fresh and bad ones in a stable rotten state. For myself, I hate to read but love to have-read. Others, however, entertain a more generous view of the role of books in our culture. Bacon noted, "We see then, how far the monuments of wit and learning are more durable than the monuments of power, or the hands. For have not the verses of Homer continued twenty-five hundred years, or more, without the loss of a syllable or letter; during which time infinite places, temples, castles, cities have been decayed and demolished?"—Francis Bacon: Advancement of Learning. Disraeli was more succinct: "A book may be as great a thing as a battle"—Benjamin Disraeli: Memoir of Isaac Disraeli.

In my lifetime, it is quite possible that new books will largely disappear from the cultural landscape as tasty internet morsels become the prevailing standard for our national attention deficit disorder. A book, however, like a spouse, demands a greater commitment and returns a greater enrichment as its reward. We will be long forgotten by the time the book has shared its destiny with the pen and typewriter.

Advice on Books and Reading

1. Read at least one non-fiction book per year throughout your life, and don't read more than one book per week (not counting books required for school). Read in diverse areas rather than merely where your interests lie.

2. When reading non-fiction, read slowly, carefully, and analyze the logic and arguments to see how they fit with your prior knowledge of your own sense of logic. The value of an idea is not elevated by virtue of being in print (Likewise, the value of the spoken word is not augmented by stentorian tones or eloquence).

3. Read the following books, beginning to end, before your 21st birthday:

        Calories & Carbohydrates (Barbra Kraus)
        Family Legal Guide (Reader's Digest)
        Foundation (Isaac Asimov)
        The Gods Themselves (Isaac Asimov)
        Webster's New World Dictionary
        The Dragons of Eden (Carl Sagan)
        Bartlet's Familiar Quotations (John Bartlet)
        Siddartha (Herman Hesse)
        On Becoming A Person (Carl Rogers)
        On the Genealogy of Morals (Friedrich Nietzche)
        How To Solve It (G. Polya)
        A New Guide to Rational Living (Ellis & Harper)
        For Yourself (Loni Barbach)
        Civilization and its Discontents (Sigmund Freud)
        The Joy of Sex (Alex Comfort)
        Man's Search for Meaning (Viktor Frankl)
        The Human Body (Isaac Asimov)
        Our Bodies, Our Selves (Boston Women's

Health Book
(Collectives)
Poor Richard's Almanac (Benjamin Franklin)
Nicomakian Ethics (Aristotle)
The Teachings of Buddha (Society for the Promotion of Buddhism)
The Christian Bible
The Koran
Guns, Germs, and Steel, The fates of Human Societies (Jared Diamond)
The Universe and Dr. Einstein (Lincoln Barnet)
Gilbert's Law Summaries (Contracts)
Capitalism and Freedom (Milton Friedman)

18 CHILDREN

Only through creative artistic, musical, or scientific activity and by the production of children can man or woman achieve immortality. Without a close second, the choice to have a child is the most important decision in a person's life. It is one of those choices which is essentially irreversible, takes little effort to execute, and potently impacts every other choice that you will make. It is a model of the rule of irreversibility and potency. That is, the care and time spent on a decision should be directly proportional to its irreversibility and potency. Because having a child is irreversible and potent, you should undertake this choice after long and diligent thought.

There was a time in human history, long before city-states developed and complex civilization became global, when it was important for everyone to reproduce and reproduce often. The survival of the species required this in light of the scarcity of resources, the attenuated lifespan, and the abundance of life-threatening adversity. Accordingly, religions and society placed strong pressures on the young to marry and reproduce often. These values and pressures continue in modern times despite the fact that the planet is crawling with humans, which in their numbers and consumptive proclivities, threaten the planet itself and all other species. It is important to keep in mind that having children is a choice, and it is not the best choice for everyone. But once you make that choice, you must surrender to its obligations. It is said, "So long as little children are allowed to suffer, there is no true love in this world"— Isadora Duncan: Dictated, Berlin, Dec. 20, 1924. Make your choice to have children one that brings joy and success. If you can't do that, or you are not ready, don't have children, or wait for readiness to signal the beginning of this special chapter in your life.

Advice on Children

1. Do not have children until you are married and have been living with your spouse for at least two years.

2. If you are planning to have children, begin trying to have them before thirty-one. Don't have children before age twenty-six. Have three or less children. Two children is best. Having one child often produces difficulties for the child and should be avoided unless medical or practical consideration dictate not having more children. Do not have extra children simply to ensure having a child of a particular sex.

3. Do not attempt to produce children unless you have a steady residence and unless you or your spouse has a steady job.

4. Never choose to have children just because you got pregnant. Do not allow yourself to get pregnant by chance. Control your life and choose to have children (rather than having them passively because that's what "happens").

5. Do not have children until both you and your spouse are clearly ready. Don't push your spouse into having children.

6. Discuss having children, especially the practicalities (like money, expectations of wife returning to work, child

care duties, etc.) for at least six months prior to trying to get pregnant.

7. Before deciding to have children, attempt to do some child care (possibly for a friend) for several days.

8. Do not have children in an attempt to save a faltering marriage. Choose to have children when your marriage is stable and secure, and your life is financially secure.

9. Before you have children, make sure that you've acted out your fantasies about wild and free fun (romantic trips, fancy dining out, geographical hopping about, etc.).

10. After the first three months of infancy, arrange for enough babysitting (by relative or paid sitter) to have one free evening per two-week period (this is a minimum).

11. If at all possible, breastfeed your children for at least the first three months of life. However, always supplement your breast feeding with one bottle of formula per day.

12. Expect that you and your spouse will differ at times about child rearing decisions. Attempt to resolve these inevitable disputes by slow, calm, non-criticizing conversation. Do not quote relatives to support your beliefs. If disputes cannot be rationally resolved, then flip a coin.

13. Child rearing (feedings, changing, etc., etc.) should be evenly divided between two working spouses in proportion to the number of hours they work (both on the job and in the home), not in proportion to the spouses' incomes.

14. Treat all advice from relatives (especially grandmothers) and friends as mere recommendations. Do not let anyone give you orders about how to raise your children. If anyone tries to control your relationship with your children, then stop allowing them in your home.

15. Always support your wife (husband) when relatives criticize her (his) childrearing decisions.

16. Don't live through your children. Don't demand that they be something you wanted to be or accomplish something that you failed to accomplish. Encourage them

to develop their own goals.

17. Don't give your children severe punishments in the heat of anger. Likewise, don't threaten punishments you won't or can't carry out. Rather, have a calm, fair, reliable set of punishments that you've set in your mind in advance. Carry out all your threats, and therefore, make reasonable threats.

18. When you decide to use physical punishment with your children, then strike them on the buttocks with your hand. Do not strike them anywhere else and do not strike them with belts, wood, or other devices.

19. Never use physical punishment more than twice in a one-month period.

20. Use physical punishment only to stop a child from doing an aggressive or dangerous act.

21. Control your children by rewarding desirable behavior with affection, smiles, verbal praise, food or toy rewards, money, and special privileges. Attempt to utilize physical affection, smiles, verbal praise, and your attention as the most common form of reward. You can also control your children by punishment, the withdrawal of rewards, and on special occasions by physical punishment.

22. No matter what your child does and no matter how angry your child makes you, always communicate, in the end, that you think your child is smart, attractive, and good. You must convey this verbally, and you must convey this often.

23. Treat your children fairly and equally. Every parent has a favorite child; this is normal, but don't let your children know this.

24. As your children get older and older, give them more and more freedom.

25. Hold, hug, cuddle, carry, and talk to your young infant as much as you possibly can. This goes for you too DAD.

26. Don't let your children (over age nine months) manipulate you with crying.

27. When infants (and small children) cry, make sure they have been fed, changed, burped, and held. Check to make sure the child is adequately warm and is in a comfortable position. If you have tried these tactics and the child is still crying, then try leaving the child alone for forty-five minutes. After age four or five months, avoid reinforcing crying behavior during the night (10 p.m. to 5 a.m.).

28. Don't scream at your children (except maybe once a week).

29. Each parent should attempt to spend some time alone with each of their children. This is especially true when your children are over five years old.

30. Give your children this book as a present when they are twelve years old.

31. As an absolute rule, your adolescent children must either go to school or to work. Never allow an adolescent to be free from one of these two responsibilities.

32. Don't ever verbally praise a boy for behaving or dressing like a girl. Never suggest that effeminate behavior is cute.

33. As your child approaches the age eighteen, try to change your relationship from a parent-child relationship to an adult-adult relationship. Try to be a friend to your older child. Attempt to slowly give up the role of protector, ruler, and supplier, allowing the emergence of the role of advisor, lender, and friend.

34. Be very careful not to be overly restrictive with adolescent children.

Dr. Rex Julian Beaber

19 DIVORCE

"Marriage is primarily a matter of mutual destiny. Marriage sets up an indissoluble state of tension, and its very existence depends upon the preservation of this state. Man and woman, both as individuals and as types, are fundamentally different, incompatible and essentially solitary. In marriage they form an indissoluble unit of life, based upon fixed distance"—Herman Alexander von Keyserling. This "unit" however dissolves with great frequency. Accordingly, almost everyone has been touched by divorce in some way. It has been said that: "The majority of great men are the offspring of unhappy marriages"— Herman Alexander von Keyserling.

Emotional divorce is not the acknowledgment of a mistake; it is a mistake not to acknowledge. If your marriage didn't hurt, then your divorce will kill you. If your divorce doesn't hurt, then your marriage will kill you.

The most frequent mistake made concerning divorce is failing to learn from the experience. This arises from engaging in blame and fault analysis, fraught with self-deception and defensiveness, rather than honest introspection. If you find yourself seeking solace and support from friends and relatives, presenting your case of victimization repeatedly, then you should assume that it is you that you are trying to convince.

Advice on Divorce

1. Don't ever mention divorce or threaten divorce as a strategy, trick, or game. Never use the word in the heat of an argument. Mention the possibility of divorce only after you've thought about it, have a clear opinion, and are emotionally calm.

2. Don't divorce your husband or wife for a single bad act, e.g., an affair, a slap, a poor financial decision, etc.

3. If you are seriously considering a divorce, do not seek individual psychotherapy or counseling. Seek counseling with your partner.

4. Before filing for divorce, see a psychotherapist for joint counseling at least three times.

5. Do not regard divorce as a personal failure or something to be ashamed of. Try your best to understand it as an incompatibility of wants, desires, and inclinations.

6. If you are considering divorce because you've fallen in love with someone with whom you are having an affair, don't mention divorce, the affair, or your dissatisfaction unless the affair has continued for six months and until you've arranged to spend several whole 24-hour days with your new love. Remember, it is always a biased comparison to compare the infatuation and titillations of a new relationship with the more sedate emotions associated with a long-term marriage.

7. Once you and your spouse have decided to get a divorce, it is essential that you proceed forward, i.e. file papers, divide property, and physically separate as rapidly as possible. Do not introduce any unnecessary delays. Don't use delays as a strategy.

8. If your spouse has gone ahead and gotten a lawyer, then you must get a lawyer immediately. Never let your spouse choose a lawyer for the both of you.

9. If at all possible, avoid lawyers and courts. Attempt to resolve all issues of monies, properties, child custody, child support, etc. on your own with a psychologist acting as a mediator. Use your sense of fairness, not technical rules of law, to resolve disputes about these issues. When you reach an agreement, then go to a lawyer who is hired by both of you (and who is mutually acceptable). Tell him that his job is to write up your agreement and expedite a speedy divorce. Remember that it is your right not to assert all of your rights.

10. Don't use demands for money, support, child custody, etc. as a means of punishing your spouse, venting anger, expiating guilt or stopping the divorce. Use the principle of fairness to resolve all problems.

11. While this is not the law, a fair division of property for a working marriage (both partners have a full-time job) is that each get back what they had prior to the marriage and all assets acquired during the marriage be divided proportionally by income. That is, if the wife earned twice as much as the husband, then she should receive 2/3 of the acquired assets. This formula doesn't work if one partner worked both outside the home (job) and significantly in the home (housekeeper, childcare, cook, gardener, etc.)

12. If you have children, then you must meet and decide how you are going to announce the divorce, and you must announce the divorce together—that is, with both parents present and all children present. Neither parent should blame the other parent or encourage the child to take sides in the divorce. During this meeting, you must answer all the children's asked and unasked questions: Where will we live? Who will we live with? When will we see you (the leaving person)? How will we survive? Will we go to the same school? Are you going to get back together again? Why is this happening?

13. A parent should never leave suddenly without talking to his children.

14. Once separation has occurred, each partner should

carry out their obligations, i.e. facilitating visitation (flexibly), paying child support, etc., exactly on time, without games or power struggles.

15. When children are involved, neither parent should ever make a promise that is not kept. The leaving parent should always arrive for visitation exactly when they say they will. No promises of trips, visits, new daddy, or anything unless you are going to come through.

16. Tell all your children, in no uncertain terms, that the divorce is not their fault. In your silence, they will often assume they are in some manner responsible.

17. If you have minimal assets and agree on most things, attempt to do the divorce by yourself. Buy a how-to-do-it divorce book. Always remember, attorneys make money by making trouble.

18. If your spouse is a chronic alcoholic, a chronic drug abuser, a person who has been charged with child molestation (if you have a child), or a habitual criminal, then divorce him/her now.

19. If you are unsure whether your husband/wife has a chronic problem like the ones in number eighteen above, then divorce him/her and live together as unmarried. If he/she is symptom free for years, then remarry. If you share children, then you'll have to periodically meet. During these meetings, focus on the business at hand. Don't talk about old resentments. Let it end.

20. After divorce, especially after being divorced, your greatest assets are your family and friends. Attempt to fill your life with dates—appointments with friends and relatives. Schedule and plan your activities a week in advance; avoid unscheduled, lonely weekends and weekday evenings. Maybe take a night class—something easy and fun.

21. After a divorce, share your confusion and depression with your friends, but don't obsess about the divorce, and don't languish in depression.

22. Don't take a vacation from work during or just after

a divorce. Work longer hours and become more involved in work.

23. Give yourself one month to be depressed after divorce; then give up your depression; try being angry, and start trying to find a new person to "date." If you have children, don't hide behind them to avoid the risks of seeing men (or women).

24. After a divorce, make a positive change in yourself that you've been postponing: lose weight, give up smoking, buy some clothes, etc.

25. Make up some view of your divorce that presents the divorce as a positive or necessary event. This is a time of emotional growth. Find some lesson in your divorce you can use to tell yourself it was worth it.

26. In general, avoid the extremes of blaming the decay of your relationship on yourself or on your spouse. It takes two people to make and destroy a relationship. Accept responsibility for your shortcomings and work on these in the future. Recognize the shortcomings of your ex-spouse as well, perhaps looking for different qualities in your next mate.

27. Avoid talking at length about your ex-spouse to friends and potential lovers. Never praise you ex or talk longingly about him/her with a new lover.

28. If the divorce is causing you depression and agitation that you can't control, then try walking five miles a day, maybe during the early evening.

29. While in the throes of divorce, don't use drugs or drink alcohol (in larger amounts than usual).

30. Just after a divorce/separation, allow yourself to cry; give yourself permission to release pent-up sadness. But, avoid being overly emotional in the presence of your children. They will need you to display some strength and self-control.

31. Avoid long separations (more than six months) when you are using separation as an experiment. After six months, get divorced or get back together. In general, do

not use separation to "help" the marriage or to "explore." Separations only unnecessarily prolong divorce and create pain/hope in the abandoned partner.

Dr. Rex Julian Beaber

20 DRUGS AND ALCOHOL

Recreational drugs are one of the only methods of changing one's mind without changing one's attitudes or opinions. Almost every culture and society that has ever existed has developed some method to be pleasantly intoxicated. Some have suggested that there may even be a biological drive to alter consciousness. One should abandon the idea that shortcuts to hedonic satisfaction are inherently evil or a sign of moral depravity. The focus should be on risks, costs, control, and functional impact.

Much of the cultural wisdom, folklore, and mythology concerning drugs has focused on the dangers of heroin, amphetamines (including cocaine), barbiturates, PCP, and pain killers. In fact, many do not appreciate that alcohol and cigarettes are by far the most dangerous drugs from a social cost point of view. Indeed, most do not think of alcohol and cigarettes as drugs (which they clearly are) simply because the delivery system is not by pill or injection. However, cloaking a chemical in a liquid delivery system or a smokable-stick does not mitigate its dangerous properties one iota.

Booth said it well:

"Drink has drained more blood, Hung more crepe,

Sold more houses,
Plunged more people into bankruptcy,
Armed more villains,
Slain more children,
Snapped more wedding rings,
Defiled more innocence,
Clouded more eyes,
Twisted more limbs,
Dethroned more reason,
Wrecked more manhood,
Dishonored more womanhood,
Broken more hearts,
Blasted more lives,
Driven more to suicide, and Dug more graves than any other poison scourge that ever swept its death-dealing waves across the world."

—Evangeline Booth: Good Housekeeping

There is a master principle regarding the taking of recreational drugs. With the exception of the verboten drugs (listed below), drugs should only be taken in small amounts, infrequently, and under circumstances where important work, love, child rearing, and safety functions are not compromised. This is the rule of moderation. The second master principle is even simpler. If you can't use in moderation, you must abstain absolutely and completely.

Advice on Drugs, Etc.

1. The general key to the wise use of drugs (alcohol, coffee, marijuana, LSD, cocaine, etc.) is control and moderation.

2. Although moderation is the general key to recreational drugs, you should never use heroin; never inject a drug; never use PCP; never use barbiturates (reds), and never, never take a drug when you are not certain about what you are taking (Note: most cities have a free service where you can anonymously submit a drug and have its

contents analyzed).

3. Don't take a drug prescribed by a physician until you have (a) memorized its name, (b) know what it's a treatment for, and (c) know what its side effects and risks are.

4. Never take recreational drugs when you feel sad, depressed, anxious and confused.

5. Take recreational drugs when you feel happy and relatively trouble-free.

6. Take recreational drugs when you have finished your work for the day.

7. Use recreational drugs: (a) after 3 p.m., (b) before a vacation day (not before a work day), (c) with one or two good friends (not in a group with unknown people, and not alone), (d) indoors or in a backyard (but not in a public place), and (e) in a situation where you won't have to drive while under the influence and where there are not environmental dangers (e.g. cliffs, pools, etc.).

8. If you take recreational drugs according to the rules stated here, then don't let anyone make you feel guilty or foolish about using drugs. Enjoy the experience and teach yourself to enjoy low doses of drugs (be a gourmet).

9. Do not ever take narcotic painkillers (Vicodin, Oxycontin, Percocet, Morphine, etc.) for any other reason than to treat actual pain caused by a medical condition or injury.

10. Avoid taking any recreational drugs before (one month) or during pregnancy. This rule applies to coffee, alcohol, grass (cannabis), aspirin, over-the-counter pain and cold remedies, and everything else. If you feel unable to do this, see a psychologist or a psychiatrist immediately.

11. Except for caffeine, don't use any drug (recreational) more than two days a week.

12. Drink wine or beer and avoid hard alcohol (whiskey, etc.).

13. Drink alcohol to get intoxicated, not to quench your thirst. If you are thirsty, drink water or a soft drink before you drink alcohol.

14. Drink alcohol before or during meals. Drink slowly so as to maintain a steady, light intoxication.

15. If you like both grass (marijuana) and alcohol and you are not sure which to use, then smoke grass (unless the legal risks are too great).

16. Don't mix drugs. Choose your pleasure for the evening and stick with it. Especially don't mix alcohol with other drugs.

17. Don't tell your children to "never use drugs." Teach the rule of moderation. Don't tell your children horror stories about drugs.

18. If you take recreational drugs in pill form or powder form (e.g., Valium, cocaine, Dexedrine), then don't take them in the presence of your children, and make sure your children can't accidentally find and use them. Don't be intoxicated in the presence of your children unless you have excellent self-control.

19. Don't take one drug to undo the unpleasant effects of another drug (e.g., a Valium to calm you down after using cocaine). 20. Use recreational drugs to enhance an experience (e.g., a meal, a movie, a talk, a game) rather than as a form of entertainment in itself (LSD is an exception to this rule).

21. If you can't follow these rules, don't use drugs. If you can't follow this rule, seek professional help.

22. If a friend wants a drug, give it to him or her; never sell drugs. But don't give drugs to friends who break the rules in this chapter.

Dr. Rex Julian Beaber

21 HOBBIES, RECREATION, AND PLEASURE

The choice of your hobbies and recreational activities is not a critical life decision. Nevertheless, these choices do have a significant impact on both your mental and physical wellbeing. Everyone could benefit from a cheap and safe obsession. In this life arena, the most ubiquitous failure is the failure to have any hobbies or sources of recreational pleasure at all. The demands of work, family obligations, basic chores, etc. often leave little time or energy for recreational pleasure.

Advice on Hobbies, Recreation, and Pleasure

1. Before age twenty-five, cultivate three hobbies. One should be a hobby that can be pursued alone, one should involve social contact, and one should involve physical activity. For these purposes, a hobby is defined broadly to include sports, games, art, and the more traditional hobbies [Examples: stamp and coin collecting, sculpting, gardening, tennis, lawn bowling, chess, model building, science fiction reading, etc., etc.]

2. Do not choose hobbies that are an extension of your work tasks. Let your hobby be a rest from work or school.

3. Pursue some activity in one of your hobbies at least once per week. Choose your hobby such that the expense of undertaking the hobby does not inhibit your regular indulgence.

4. Do not undertake more than one hobby that is competitive, and undertake at least one hobby where your performance will be ordinary. You should not place yourself in a situation where all of your hobbies trigger intense achievement motivation.

Dr. Rex Julian Beaber

22 TRAVEL AND VACATION

Do we have enough money? Do you have the tickets? What clothes should I take? Carting around luggage, rushing, waiting, photographing, coordinating reservations, functioning while sleep deprived, worrying about the house, the pets, the job, dealing with exchange rates and foreign languages, wrestling with taxi cab drivers, and all the rest. Ah, the joys of travel. In actuality, there are no ardors of travel that a fast jet, a servant, more time, and infinite money would not solve. A vacation is wishing it would never end; fun is not knowing what time it is.

Expressed as a percentage of your life span, vacation time reflects a small portion of life. Your vacation choices are not Critical Life Decisions, and for thousands of years, human civilizations had no vacation time for the working class. Unfortunately, this special time is often a source of misery and profound stress (Much of the stress reflects time pressures and the unexpected financial costs of travel). Vacations have the potential to produce interesting experiences and memories, with some rejuvenation and refreshment. But without some wisdom in preparation, they can degenerate into an unpleasant labor. Finding the proper balance, for you, in the elements of rest and rejuvenation versus stimulation, challenge, and novelty is not easy, and it is often made more difficult because your vacation partners, including children, mate, or friends, may have significantly different needs for stimulation and rest. Indeed, your choice of vacation companions may be a more important choice than your choice of vacation destinations. As a general rule, unless you have an established history of vacation harmony with a travel companion, you should not plan a long vacation with anyone until you have attempted a few short trips. Vacation travel creates a level of twenty-four-hour proximity and intimacy that can be a challenge even for couples or families that otherwise live in tranquility.

Advice on Travel and Vacation

1. Arrange, when taking a travel vacation, to have a whole day at home before returning to work. Try also to have a full day at home before leaving. This will remove a lot of travel stress.

2. If you travel to a foreign country, arrange to get your passport at least six months prior to leaving.

3. When traveling to foreign countries, arrange to have several hundred dollars' worth of the foreign currency in your pocket (not your luggage), before your arrival. Don't get on that plane without foreign currency. Be sure that currency includes some small bills for payment of taxi fares upon arrival.

4. When traveling to foreign countries, carry traveler's checks (or the equivalent). Change your checks into foreign currency slowly on a day-by-day basis. You should carry with you on vacation at least two credit cards. You should not have all of your cash, credit cards, and traveler's checks stored in the same place. They should be divided between several bags, a zippered pocket, a purse (for women), and a secured pocket. Essentially, do not place yourself in a position where one lost bag can destroy your vacation because it has all your monetary resources. Likewise, don't

place yourself in a situation where a pickpocket can destroy your vacation by taking all your credit cards, money, or crucial identification.

5. Take luxurious vacations. That is, don't plan to use all your money on as many days as possible; rather, shorten the vacation, and live high. Overestimate the costs of your vacation and be prepared to live with that cost.

6. Save and pay for your vacation in advance; don't travel on credit.

7. Keep your vacation simple. Specifically, a) take as little luggage as possible, b) go to very few cities, c) avoid spending days getting on and off of trains, planes, etc. Have a few planned activities each day but reserve a little rest time and unplanned time.

8. Avoid vacations that begin and end with long car rides. Plan your vacation with less than four hours car travel in any one day. Split long rides between two days (doing some sightseeing in between).

9. Take vacations during off times; that is, avoid popular spots when they are overcrowded. Try to take your vacation at a non-traditional time or season. Throughout the year, there are a number of three-day weekends (e.g., Memorial Day, etc.). Don't travel on these days. Make these holidays home holidays. Choose some other Friday or Monday and take your vacation then (Other holidays can also be celebrated on a different day than the holiday to save money and avoid crowds).

10. Don't travel to foreign countries that have minimal civil rights, politically unstable governments, or known hostile relationships with your home country (e.g., the U.S.). In general, be very careful about traveling to Central and South America, the Middle East, Africa, and the former Soviet Union.

11. When in foreign countries, don't make political statements or participate in protests, and don't break any law (no matter how minor). Don't carry packages or luggage at anyone's request.

12. When traveling to a foreign country, carry with you a translation dictionary.

13. When traveling, tip well, be very nice, and don't flash around money. Don't brag about your home country, and don't make comparisons between your home country and the country you are visiting.

14. Buy plane tickets far in advance (several months) of your departure date. Make hotel reservations far in advance and confirm them forty-eight hours before departure (by phone). Use the internet to shop for hotels and flights.

15. If you travel by car, then:
1. Get an oil change before you leave.
2. Replace all bad tires and make sure you've got a good spare.
3. Carry some kind of auto club card (for towing and emergency).
4. Fill your tank before it drops below the ¼ full mark. Don't drive on that last quarter; go to a gas station.

16. When leaving on a vacation, arrange for a neighbor to pick up your mail and newspaper. Leave an inside light on in your house, and of course, lock your doors and windows.

17. Before having your first child, take a luxurious dream trip with your spouse. This may be your last such trip for awhile.

18. It is better to take three vacations per year: two short vacations (say three or four-day weekends) and a moderate length vacation (say 7-10 days) rather than one long vacation.

19. Don't travel away from home just because you think that's the way you have to take a vacation. Sometimes it's fun to vacation in your home city. Unplug your phone, tell people you'll be away for a short trip and eat out every meal—it's great fun!

20. If you and your spouse disagree about where to travel to, then first try to compromise; if that doesn't work, try a trade ("I'll go to Paris if you'll agree to a short trip to

San Francisco before the end of this year"). If that doesn't work, try flipping a coin. Don't go on vacation with someone who is going to resent you for making them go.

21. Avoid traveling with young children unless it is unavoidable. When your children are young, take home-vacations or travel to nearby towns within four hours driving distance.

22. Before you take a significant vacation, create a Trip Document. This document should have your name, passport number, driver's license number, cell phone number, and email address. It should also have the cell number for your travel partner and an emergency contact number back home. Next, in the EXACT chronological order of the trip, the Trip Document should contain every flight (with complete information on airport, departure time, and gate), train ride, hotel (with address, confirmation number, phone number etc.). A copy of this document should be in each bag, and every adult traveler should have a copy of this document on their person.

23. Each adult should be traveling with a cell phone that will work in all countries and locations on the trip.

24. Don't to forget to take all medications that you may need on your trip with you.

23 EDUCATION

"A human being is not, in any proper sense, a human being till he is educated"—Horace Mann. One of the most important differences between homo sapiens and "lower" species in the phyla is how much must be done after birth to prepare for survival. After its metamorphosis and emergence from its cocoon, a butterfly is virtually ready for all of its life functions within seconds. In sharp contrast, in a modern society, it would not be unusual for a person to spend seventeen years in school before cultural readiness could be declared. We are not hardwired, and the potential for post-conception programming makes our capacity for adaption and creativity virtually limitless. This being said, learning can be filled with drudgery and psychological pain. It's not surprising that many flee from the arms of formal education as soon as the state will set them free. Therefore, true education must first free man from the chains of ignorance, and then free man from his educators.

Advice on Education

1. Don't go to school (college) to discover yourself or to find an occupation; rather, go to college with a specific career objective in mind.

2. At college or university don't major in the following subjects: history, English, art, sociology, music, political science, ethnic studies, or psychology unless you know that you must major in these subjects to pursue your chosen career (e.g., the career line of history professor). Pursue these areas as minor or elective courses. Major in areas that emphasize occupational skills and preparation like mathematics, all of the sciences, engineering, computer science, nursing, pharmacy, accounting, and business.

3. Pursue two different areas of study in college and study them intensely (e.g., computer science and journalism). Make sure one of your majors is quite practical in terms of job possibilities.

4. Avoid private, expensive schools (unless your career objective is politics or marriage to the wealthy), and go to good, inexpensive public universities.

5. Go to college with the intent of doing superbly; study very hard, study before playing, and distribute your studying over the entire semester rather than cramming. Plan to do all required reading three times (slowly) before exams. Finish all term papers well before the end of a semester.

6. Try to distribute your hard and difficult course work evenly such that no given semester is overly easy or hard. When in doubt, conquer difficult courses first, rewarding yourself with easy courses later.

7. Choose professors to talk to and ask them questions that indicate you're thinking beyond the scope of the lectures and text. Study beyond just getting good grades; struggle to deeply understand.

8. Cultivate friendships with faculty in the discipline closest to your future occupation.

9. Avoid fraternities, political groups, religious groups, etc. that distract you from excellence in your course work.

10. Use recreational drugs only on weekends and only after your work is finished. Save these as self-rewards.

11. Avoid outside jobs when in college. It is better to live modestly and use the time to study, think and grow.

12. Throughout school, from grammar school to college or trade school, compete against yourself or a high standard, not against siblings and friends.

13. Don't' go to college to please your parents. If you can't see college as aiding you in your goals, then go to work. Likewise, don't go to college for social approval of peers. There are many interesting forms of education in life and the working world which are just as important.

14. Do whatever is necessary to graduate from high school.

15. In either junior high school or high school, take a course in typing; it's an invaluable tool.

16. Use high school and junior high as a time to explore different careers or academic futures. Take a good variety of courses. This is a good time to do some volunteer work or part time work to get exposed to different areas.

17. Avoid the junior high and high school trap of spending all your time trying to get your friends' approval. Keep a separate identity.

18. No matter what your occupational goals, use junior high and high school to master arithmetic skills, especially to solve "word problems."

19. Make friends with at least two teachers and two students at your school.

20. Don't get a job to buy a car while in high school, unless you are not planning to attend college. On the other hand, if you're not going to college, then get a car and a job as soon as possible.

21. High school should be thought of as your last chance to be a child; have fun, don't work too hard, and prepare your mind for the next step, which is hard work.

22. Take advantage of your junior high and high school clubs, gym, etc. to find a sport you like.

23. Parents should avoid helping their children with their homework.

24. Parents should avoid trying to control their children's major or subject choices. Share your opinion and

reasons once or at most twice and then drop the subject.

25. Parents should never punish a child for their academic grades. Parents should give brief verbal (not monetary) rewards for good grades.

26. Parents should not control whether, when, or how their children will do homework.

27. Parents should convey a belief to their children that they can do well if they try hard. Parents should convey a belief that children are bright.

28. Parents should offer their children a musical education before age nine. They should encourage the playing of instruments but must let the child choose the instrument and kind of music. Reward practice and push lightly.

29. Parents should not support their child through college unless their child's performance is very superior. Each semester's support should depend on performance during the last semester. Parents of more limited income should not feel obliged to pay for their children's college education. If your child doesn't respond thankfully for college aid, discontinue it.

30. Don't send your child to a religious private school for their general education.

31. When studying: Study for twenty minutes and then take ten-minute rest breaks, repeating this cycle until several hours have passed, and then take a half-hour rest break. While studying, give 100% concentration; while resting, do something fun and rewarding.

32. Have a special place, at home or in a library, where you study; try to do nothing but studying there. Use this place as a sanctuary

.

24 IDENTIFICATION, DOCUMENTS, AND SAVING THINGS

Notwithstanding the internet and computers, we live in a world of paper. Having the right paper or document in the right place and at the right time will make the business of life flow more easily.

Advice on Identification, Documents, and Saving Things

1. At all times, carry with you a valid driver's license, two credit cards, a check guarantee card, one-hundred dollars, and the business card of your personal physician. If you possess medical insurance, your insurance card should also be on your person.
2. Get and keep a valid passport. Make sure to renew it regularly so that it remains valid.
3. Get and keep in a safe place your birth certificate.
4. Keep a file, on a year to year basis, of all cancelled checks and receipts for major purchases (purchases over $50.00). Keep this file for ten years in a safe place.
5. Have a separate file for product warranty statements and save all product warranty statements.
6. Create a legal file. In this file keep all legal documents

(e.g., divorce decrees, deeds, wills, etc.).

7. If you are over the age of thirty write a will and make sure its existence is known to at least two good friends. If your total worth (assets) exceeds a few thousand dollars, make sure to consult an attorney and create a revocable living trust.

8. Create a medical file. In this file, place insurance forms and insurance information, medical information you've been told or given by your physician, and any other medical data you may need.

9. Save all photographs of yourself and your significant others (family, friends, children, etc.) and all photographs of prior residences. In general, don't throw out photographs. The only exception to this is photographs of ex-wives and husbands. Throw all these out except for one or two to be placed in a sealed envelope.

10. Don't sign any document you don't understand. Attempt to read every document you sign. Don't be pushed into quickly signing anything. Delay signing, take the document home or to a lawyer, and think about it.

11. Seek an outside opinion before signing any document that significantly affects your property, money, stocks, or possessions.

12. Don't sign any document for home repairs or construction that places a lien against your home for failure to pay.

13. Save for each of your children (assuming you're going to have children) a copy of the daily newspaper issued on their day of birth and a copy of a weekly news magazine issued on the week of their birth. Also save several bottles of wine dated in the year of their birth (make sure the wine is of the type that improves with age).

14. Keep a special file on each of your children. In this file save birth records, medical data (immunizations, etc.), school records (especially the name and address of the schools attended), and other important documents.

15. Throw away any book that you have not read unless

you have an immediate plan to read it. Save only books that you have actually read or are used for reference purposes.

16. If you ever lose great deal of weight (enough to change your clothing size) throw away all the clothing in your old size. If you gain a large amount of weight, however, save all your old clothing and store it in the closet you regularly use.

17. Before throwing away clothes, furniture, etc., check to see if the items can be donated to some charity.

18. In a safe place, save old phone and address books.

19. In a special file, save all letters written to you, especially letters about business.

20. Make sure all oral promises are in writing before signing a contract.

21. Purchase a scanner and scan all your important documents, and store them in your computer in files that will make discovery easy. Periodically, at least once every six months, make a backup file, on a disk, thumb drive, or other out-of-computer storage device, of your important documents. In addition to computer storage, keep a hard copy of your critical documents.

22. Create, and regularly update, a single electronic document that contains the following information: Your name, telephone number, address, email address, driver's license number, passport number, telephone number, fax number, a list of all of your credit card numbers, a list of the contact information of your close relatives, three best friends, and your personal physician, your health and home insurance policy numbers, a list of your current medications (with dosage) and each of your active medical diagnoses, your car insurance information, and, in some coded format, your various passwords. Regarding your passwords, it is absolutely imperative that they be stored in some coded manner such that if someone got access to your document, they could not use the passwords.

Dr. Rex Julian Beaber

25 LAW AND LEGAL AFFAIRS

There are few life domains where our sentiments are so conflicted and paradoxical as law, lawyers, and legal affairs. These divergent points of view are shared by the great minds of our time. Aristotle praised the law: "The law is reason free from passion"—Aristotle: Politics, bk. 3. Alternatively, Burke feared its power: "Bad laws are the worst sort of tyranny"—Edmund Burke. Others have focused on the class bias in all laws. "The fine spider web of the law catches the fly and lets hawk go through"—Spanish Proverb.

In fact, modern law with its complexities is a relatively recent evolutionary development of human societies. From our early tribal beginnings until the development of city-states, the rule of power dominated human affairs. In a global transvaluation of morals, religions created rules that slowly replaced the purely power-based ordering of society. In the twentieth century, law replaces religion as the primary tool for taming the wild beast in man. This has generated a growing view of law as a necessary evil. "We, like the eagles, were born to be free. Yet we are obliged, in order to live at all, to make a cage of laws for ourselves and to stand on the perch"—William Bolitho: Twelve Against the Gods.

Accordingly, a common perspective now is on the nuance of constructing laws that result in perceptibly fair and orderly resolution of conflict. "It is a very easy thing to devise good laws; the difficulty is to make them effective. The great mistake is that of looking upon men as virtuous, or thinking that they can be made so by laws; and consequently, the greatest art of a politician is to render vices serviceable to the cause of virtue"—Henry S. John Bolingbroke.

A part of the ambivalence towards the law arises from its apparent cryptic and esoteric character. In fact, however, there really are no difficult ideas in the law, just a morass of unfamiliar vocabulary calculated to create the impression of a subtle science when only common sense is at play. Make a respectable effort, and you will penetrate the cloak of vocabulary.

A few areas of law are responsible for the majority of legal principles that ordinary people need to know. They are: (a) the laws of marital property and child custody; (b) the law of contracts; (c) a little bit of the law of wills and trusts; and (d) the general laws of negligence liability. These legal arenas vary a bit from state-to-state. They are not difficult to understand with some effort, and a basic appreciation of these legal areas will greatly enhance your life. It is shocking that millions of people graduate high school being able to solve algebraic simultaneous equations, which they will never use as an adult, and yet are ignorant of the basics of law in these important domains. It would be wise for everyone to read a summary, applicable to their state, of the basic areas of law before they attain the age of twenty-one. Additionally, given the amount of discourse in the public sector, it would also be good to read the U.S. Constitution, end-to-end, a few times, and think about it. This later task could be accomplished in an hour or two.

Advice on Law and Lawyers

1. Avoid hiring lawyers to do minor legal tasks like evictions, small suits, and divorces. Try to read up and do these yourself; it's easier than you think, and it's rarely cost effective to use a lawyer (unless very large sums of money are involved).

2. Don't break the law unless you do so out of a deep moral conviction (and are willing to live with the consequences) or unless you are committing a victimless crime (e.g., using an illegal drug).

3. If you are charged with a crime, hire an attorney who has worked for a number of years as a public defender. If you lack funds to hire an attorney, use the public defender. Do not defend yourself if you are charged with a felony. If you are arrested and charged with a crime or taken for questioning regarding a crime, assert your right to remain silent and to have an attorney present. Regardless of whether you are guilty or innocent, do not waive your Miranda right to remain silent.

4. When hiring a lawyer, search for someone who is young and who is not so successful and rich so as to regard your case as unimportant. A hungry lawyer in a civil action is your best bet.

5. Be open to resolving civil actions (suits) out of Court for less money than you want.

6. Whenever hiring an attorney be clear with him about exactly how much money he charges and exactly what you are going to get for that money. Attempt to hire a lawyer to finish a task (paying for the complete task) rather than hiring a lawyer by time. Pay the smallest retainer possible (make sure considerable amounts of the fee are payable after he does his work).

7. Don't file a lawsuit just to vent anger. Beware of attorneys who take advantage of your anger to induce you to engage in expensive and unnecessary legal actions.

8. Don't ever try to help a friend by telling a lie for him

to a law enforcement officer.

9. If you are a witness to a crime, do not exaggerate the sureness of your memory, and don't feel pressured to identify people in line-ups.

10. If you are present when a crime is committed, be calm, try to memorize information that will help police (e.g., license plate numbers, facial features, type of gun, etc., etc.). Use this focus to help yourself remain calm.

11. If you are a victim of a crime, follow the advice in #10 above and calmly search for a way to escape the situation. Don't attempt to escape without thinking it through and being fairly sure that you'll make it. Never verbally assault a criminal during a crime. Never physically attack a criminal during a crime unless: a) you are fairly sure your life is in danger or b) you are very sure that you will win.

12. If you are a victim of a crime, report the crime and cooperate with the investigation and prosecution. Women, this especially goes for rape and other sex crimes.

13. When hiring a lawyer to do a complex task, make sure you hire someone who has handled a similar case before.

14. Don't support propositions to change the law unless you have carefully analyzed the pros and cons. Be especially careful about supporting new laws when they are introduced in response to some single case or episode or some current emotional issue.

15. Don't take the law into your own hands and try to personally produce justice. Solve your problems with people by using the legal process rather than through your own action. Don't commit a crime to avenge a crime.

16. Calmly threatening to file a lawsuit, or better, having an attorney send a letter to this effect, often produces wonders for very little money. Use threat, but use it in an adult way—calm, cold, deliberate, and unexaggerated.

17. The most frequent mistake people make in their legal affairs is failing to create written agreements when

dealing in business and personal financial transactions. Clear written agreements would eliminate most legal disputes in business and personal financial affairs. This is especially true for ongoing relationships, like joint ventures and partnerships, or in deals between friends and relatives (which are generally unwise). Whenever you get involved in a significant business or financial transaction, you should think through and draft a detailed written agreement that covers all promises, duties, performances, and conditions. If the agreement involves something very important or a great deal of money, then it is worth it to retain a lawyer. Do not substitute trust, friendship, or informality for a detailed written agreement. Make sure the agreement is signed, scanned, saved, and honored. If during the course of the agreement, changes are negotiated, confirm them in WRITING. Generally, it is wise to have agreements sent via the internet where there will be a clear record of the source, time, and transmission of the agreement.

18. Anyone who has significant wealth should enter into a written and enforceable prenuptial agreement before marriage which, among other things, lists exhaustively your separate property. This is one of those tasks that does require an attorney.

19. Don't sign a contract or agreement you haven't read.

20. If you are over forty-five years old, have significant money, or a dependent child, have an attorney draft a revocable living trust to handle the disposition of your assets upon your death or disability.

21. In the event of a divorce, do not involve yourself in a child custody dispute to vent your anger at your spouse or to secure greater post-divorce support. Don't use your child to hurt your spouse, don't denigrate your spouse, and reserve child custody proceedings to protect a child from physical abuse, body-threatening negligence, and SEVERE psychological abuse. Otherwise, work cooperatively to have roughly equal custodial time in a mutually respectful manner.

26 LYING AND DECEIT

Lies, and especially liars, have been universally demonized through the ages, notwithstanding that lies are the lubricant that keeps the machinery of social, family, and business life running without undue interpersonal friction. Truth, alternatively, is almost always treated as a meta-virtue. Indeed, truth itself is regarded as a victim. "The men that American people admire most extravagantly are the most daring liars; the men they detest most violently are those who try to tell them the truth"—H.L. Mencken: The Vintage Mencken, edited by Alistair Cook, Knopf, p. 73.

Some pundits, however, appreciate that truth may be overrated. "A truth that's told with bad intent; Beats all the lies you can invent"—William Blake: Auguries of Innocence. Some literal truths are recognized as more devilish than straightforward prevarication. "There are three kinds of lies: Lies, damned lies, and statistics"—Benjamin Disraeli: Attributed by Mark Twain, Autobiography. Indeed, even attempting to neither lie nor speak the truth does not immunize one from moral critique. "The cruelest lies are often told in silence"—Robert Louis Stevenson: Vigiribus Pureisque.

Acknowledging that lies are a must of social intercourse,

others have focused on an imaginary typology of lies. A classification as a "white" lie is an especially potent justifier. Of course, everybody tells white lies. The lies that everybody tells me are the other kind of lies. A wiser evaluation of lying looks to the function of the lie and what it facilitates. In the final analysis, Holmes was right: "Sin has many tools, but a lie is the handle that fits them all"— Oliver Wendell Holmes (Sr.): The Autocrat of the Breakfast Table. It is the underlying "sin" the lie facilitates that must be evaluated, because in the final analysis, a lie is as large as the evil that results from it. When a good results from a lie, it has all the virtues of truth, and indeed, it may bespeak a better man. "Any fool can tell the truth, but it requires a man of some sense to know how to lie well"—Samuel Butler: Note-Books. This being true, you must be prepared to be revealed; for most lies never live to be old. (Paraphrase of Sophocles: Acrisius, Fragment 59).

Advice on Lying

1. Struggle not to lie to your wife, your best friend, your psychotherapist, your physician, and your children.

2. Don't lie for the purpose of hurting someone.

3. Use lies, in the form of excuses, when you wish to decline social invitations; this will save you from unnecessarily hurting people.

4. When you lie, lie skillfully. When lying, avoid complexities (keep it simple), avoid saying things that can be verified or shown to be false, utilize some truth, and avoid creating a situation where you'll have to tell another lie to cover for the first lie.

5. Don't lie in order to make yourself look important. Specifically, don't lie about your skills, heritage, money, or power.

6. During job interviews, don't be afraid to lie about your health, your age, your future plans, or your prior history (e.g., prison or mental hospital record).

7. Don't endorse any value system that requires that you always be honest. Accept the necessity of lying periodically.

8. Shortly after telling a lie, change the subject. The longer you talk about the lie, the more likely it is that you'll make the lie detectable.

9. Don't ever lie to yourself. Don't fall into the trap of believing the lies you've told others.

10. Attempt to plan your lies rather than making them up on the spot. When planning a lie, ask yourself if there is any way it could be shown that your statement was false.

11. When you suspect that you have been lied to by anyone other than your wife or best friend, avoid confronting that person with the lie. Attempt to let the person know through your non-verbal behavior (your look of suspiciousness) that you know they are lying.

12. Don't expect or demand that everyone be truthful with you. Assume that any statement could be a lie or a half-truth. Trust your intuitive sense that some statement is a lie.

13. Assume any statement that implies a person is doing something for you (without some expected return) is a lie.

14. When you've been told something you suspect is a lie, avoid unnecessarily repeating it or giving it free circulation. You are as much a liar for having knowingly repeating a lie as if you constructed it yourself.

15. Never assume that because a person has been honest in one matter that he will be honest in all other matters. Keep in mind there are few liars, but many situations that call for a lie.

Dr. Rex Julian Beaber

27 RELIGION

When science is done, all that will be left is "Why?" This shall be the exclusive and proper domain of religion. "Religion is a daughter of Hope and Fear, explaining to Ignorance the nature of the Unknowable"—Paraphrase of Ambrose Bierce: The Devil's Dictionary.

Not surprisingly, even the greatest of scientist sees some role for religion. "If I were personally to define religion, I would say that it is a bandage that man has invented to protect a soul made bloody by circumstances. Science without religion is lame, religion without science is blind"— Albert Einstein: The World As I see It, Philosophical Library. Einstein's view, which asserts a human role in the creation of religion, is a nakedly pragmatic approach because it insinuates that a deity is not behind the beliefs, and yet claims a purpose to religion. This view was published long before Einstein. "Religion is regarded by the common people as true, by the wise as false, and by the rulers as useful"—Senca. While many appreciate the utility of religion, regardless of its underlying truth, a strong minority warn of its dangers. "We have enough religion to make us hate, but not enough to make us love one another"—Jonathan Swift: Thoughts on Various Subjects.

Others go so far as to suggest that religion cloaks actual evil. "A religion that requires persecution to sustain it is of the devil's propagation" —Hosea Ballou.

A simple statistical truth about organized religion speaks volumes about its place in society. Overwhelmingly, albeit not always, a child's religion, on becoming an adult, shall be the religion of his parents. Typically, Christians beget Christians, and Muslims sire Muslims. Lest one believe that religious fidelity is genetic, it is difficult to escape the conclusion that religious belief is typically the consequence of social influence, persuasion, modeling, and/or propaganda. We typically acquire our religious persuasion as we acquired our native tongue—not as a rational choice nor as a wondrous inspired revelation.

If one religion reflects the true nature of god and his dictates, then the only sage advice is to follow that religion dutifully. Not gifted with this insight, I shall simply give advice based on the social and psychological consequences of various religion practices.

Advice on Religion

1. Don't participate in any religious ritual unless you understand its meaning and believe in its purpose.

2. Avoid the following religions: Dianetics (aka Scientology), very strict Catholicism, Nishryn Sho Shin Buddhism, Ultra-Orthodox Judaism, Moonys, Hari Krishna, and small cults with charismatic leaders who control the minutia of the lives of their followers.

3. Never presume that anyone knows more about God than you. Don't accept leadership from people who believe they are God or who believe that God communicates with them personally and exclusively.

4. Accept religious beliefs or advice as potential sources of human wisdom that should be considered like all others based on merit. Don't reject or accept an idea narrowly based on its religious origin.

5. View God as an entity that will not help you, hurt you, or personally intervene in your life. Be prepared to accept responsibility for your life and the consequences of your choices.

6. Never deny the existence of mysteries in the Universe. Allow yourself, whether a believer in God or not, to experience the religious feelings of awe at the elegant complexity of the Universe.

7. Either practice your religion every day or not at all.

8. Do not involve yourself in religions that use the concept of evil as an explanation for all unpleasant events.

9. If you are very religious, don't marry a non-religious person or a person whose religious beliefs are clearly different than yours (and vice versa).

10. Don't try to persuade people by argument in religious matters. Persuade by being an example of a happy, wise, and ethical person.

11. Be tolerant of other people's sincere beliefs. Don't criticize people for religious beliefs that don't intrude on your life or otherwise cause harm.

12. Don't participate in religious cults that require you to terminate your relationships with friends and family and/or limit your contacts to only cult members.

13. Don't become sexually involved with a religious leader of your faith, especially your leader.

14. Don't give more than 10% of your annual income to a religious organization.

15. Don't pressure your spouse or children to practice a particular religion.

28 MISCELLANEOUS THOUGHTS, OBSERVATIONS, AND RULES

It is rare that idiocy, i.e., a lack of cognitive skill, is the reason for failure or frustration in life. Indeed, an entirely average person has remarkable intellectual resources. Most often, the problem with adverse life decisions is not impoverished thought; it is the lack of any thinking at all. Developing the habit of devoted and intense thinking before actions and decisions will allow you to triumph in life. Alternatively, even a highly gifted person who is well educated will ultimately misstep if he acts impulsively without thought.

Dr. Rex Julian Beaber

29 USEFUL QUOTATIONS

"Oh, what a tangled web we weave, when first we practise to deceive!"—Sir Walter Scott, Marmion, Canto vi. Stanza 17. Scottish author & novelist (1771 - 1832)

"Laws, like the spider's web, catch the fly and let the hawk go free"—Spanish Proverb

"I have never killed a man, but I have read many obituaries with great pleasure."— Clarence Darrow

"He has never been known to use a word that might send a reader to the dictionary."—William Faulkner (about Ernest Hemingway)

"I've had a perfectly wonderful evening. But this wasn't it."—Groucho Marx

"I didn't attend the funeral, but I sent a nice letter saying I approved of it."— Mark Twain

"He has no enemies but is intensely disliked by his friends."—Oscar Wilde

"I am enclosing two tickets to the first night of my new play; bring a friend... If you have one."—George Bernard Shaw to Winston Churchill ...followed by:

Churchill's response: "Cannot possibly attend first night, will attend second, if there is one."—Winston Churchill

"I feel so miserable without you; it's almost like having

you here."—Stephen Bishop

"He is a self-made man and worships his creator."—John Bright

"I've just learned about his illness. Let's hope it's nothing trivial."—Irvin S. Cobb

"He is not only dull himself; he is the cause of dullness in others."—Samuel Johnson

"He is simply a shiver looking for a spine to run up."—Paul Keating

"He had delusions of adequacy."—Walter Kerr

"Why do you sit there looking like an envelope without any address on it?"— Mark Twain

"His mother should have thrown him away and kept the stork."—Mae West

"Some cause happiness wherever they go; others, whenever they go."—Oscar Wilde

Lady Astor once remarked to Winston Churchill at a Dinner Party, "Winston, if you were my husband, I would poison your coffee!" Winston replied, "Madam if I were your husband I would drink it!"

Lady Astor looked at Churchill and said, "Sir, you are drunk!" He replied, "And Madam, you are ugly. At least in the morning I'll be sober."

"Eternal Vigilance is the Price of Liberty"—Michael S. Klein

Einstein quotes

"You spend thirty minutes with a beautiful girl, it seems like a moment. You spend a moment sitting on a hot stove, it seems like thirty minutes." (giving the most practical, understandable explanation of the Theory of Relativity; how time can expand or contract)

"The secret to creativity is knowing how to hide your sources."

"I do not much believe in education. Each man ought to be his own model, however frightful that may be."

"Few are those who see with their own eyes and feel with their own hearts."

"I never think of the future. It comes soon enough."

"The most beautiful thing we can experience is the mysterious."

"If we knew what it was we were doing, it would not be called research, would it?"

"The wireless telegraph is not difficult to understand. The ordinary telegraph is like a very long cat. You pull the tail in New York, and it meows in Los Angeles. The wireless is the same, only without the cat."

"Imagination is more important than knowledge. Knowledge is limited. Imagination encircles the world."

"The pursuit of truth and beauty is a sphere of activity in which we are permitted to remain children all our lives."

"There is a race between mankind and the universe. Mankind is trying to build bigger, better, faster, and more foolproof machines. The universe is trying to build bigger, better, and faster fools. So far the universe is winning."

"As a young man, my fondest dream was to become a geographer. However, while working in the customs office I thought deeply about the matter and concluded that it was far too difficult a subject. With some reluctance, I then turned to physics as a substitute."

"Only two things are infinite, the universe and human stupidity, and I'm not sure about the former."

"I assert that the cosmic religious experience is the strongest and the noblest driving force behind scientific research."

"I think and think for months and years. Ninety-nine times, the conclusion is false. The hundredth time I am right."

"When I examine myself and my methods of thought, I come close to the conclusion that the gift of fantasy has meant more to me than my talent for absorbing positive knowledge."

"I made one great mistake in my life —when I signed

the letter to President Roosevelt recommending that atom bombs be made ... but there was some justification — the danger that the Germans would make them." [Quoted by Ted Morgan in the book 'FDR', Simon & Schuster, 1985]

"The grand aim of all science is to cover the greatest number of empirical facts by logical deduction from the smallest number of hypotheses or axioms." [quoted in Life magazine, 9 January 1950]

"Whoever undertakes to set himself up as a judge of Truth and knowledge is shipwrecked by the laughter of the gods."

(Upon learning of the atomic bombing of Hiroshima): "If I had only known, I would have been a locksmith!"

"Generations to come, it may be, we'll scarcely believe that such a one as this ever in flesh and blood walked upon this earth!" (Referring to Mahatma Gandhi after Gandhi was assassinated)

"Great spirits have always encountered violent opposition from mediocre minds."

"I am a deeply religious nonbeliever. This is a somewhat new kind of religion."

"The important thing is not to stop questioning."

"Reality is merely an illusion, albeit a very persistent one."

"The difference between stupidity and genius is that genius has its limits."

"Science without religion is lame, religion without science is blind."

"Common sense is the collection of prejudices acquired by age eighteen."

"Logic will get you from A to B. Imagination will take you everywhere."

"I know not with what weapons World War III will be fought, but World War IV will be fought with sticks and stones."

"There are only two ways to live your life. One is as though nothing is a miracle. The other is as though everything is a miracle."

"If the facts don't fit the theory, change the facts."

"An empty stomach is not a good political adviser."

"Education is what remains after one has forgotten everything he learned in school."

"The hardest thing in the world to understand is income tax."

30 ABOUT THE AUTHOR

Dr. Beaber's background and training reflect a peripatetic journey through intellectual diversity. He was originally trained as a clinical and forensic psychologist, and then later he trained as a lawyer specializing in criminal and civil trials. His social commentary has appeared in major and minor news publications, and he has often served as an analyst for various TV docudramas.

More specifically, Dr. Beaber did his undergraduate work at UCLA and then received this masters and doctoral degrees in Clinical Psychology at USC. He spent one year as a psychology intern at the Long Beach Veterans Hospital, followed by a one-year fellowship in clinical psychology at Cedars Sinai Medical Center. After this, he undertook a second fellowship in the Department of Psychiatry at the USC Medical School.

After his formal training, Dr. Beaber spent a short time as the director of a county mental health program in Ventura Country, followed by his acceptance of a faculty position teaching in the General Medicine/ Family Medicine residency-training program and the UCLA Medical School. While teaching, seeing patients, and doing some limited research, Dr. Beaber consulted with prosecutors, courts, and defense counsel on the mental states of serial killers, sex offenders, and other sociopathic offenders.

After developing a reputation as an accomplished expert

witness, Beaber abruptly changed course and began studying law. He graduated Order of Coif and as an Editor of the UCLA Law Review from UCLA Law School. After, training under two federal judges, he went on to practice law in the areas of complex business civil litigation and criminal defense for many years, trying cases in both state and federal court. Additionally, he served as the outside general counsel to a publicly traded company.

In the final analysis, however, Beaber believes his greatest accomplishment has been raising and nurturing his two children. His daughter is a delightful and wise psychologist in Northern California. His son is an intellectually diverse neurologist specializing in multiple sclerosis, who has created a nuclear family with two children that would be any father's delight.

www.ingramcontent.com/pod-product-compliance
Lightning Source LLC
Chambersburg PA
CBHW020418080526
44584CB00014B/1381